The Procrastination Fix

36 Strategies Proven To Cure Laziness And Improve Productivity

Daily Training For Mental Toughness And Self Discipline

Jacob Greene

© Copyright 2018 by Jacob Greene - All rights reserved.

This document is geared towards providing exact and reliable information in regards to the topic and issue covered. The publication is sold with the idea that the publisher is not required to render accounting, officially permitted, or otherwise, qualified services. If advice is necessary, legal or professional, a practiced individual in the profession should be ordered.

From a Declaration of Principles which was accepted and approved by a Committee of the American Bar Association and a Committee of Publishers and Associations.

In no way is it legal to reproduce, duplicate, or transmit any part of this document in either electronic means or in printed format. Recording of this publication is strictly prohibited and any storage of this document is not allowed unless with written permission from the publisher. All rights reserved.

The information provided herein is stated to be truthful and consistent, in that any liability, in terms of inattention or otherwise, by any usage or abuse of any policies, processes, or directions contained within is the solitary and utter responsibility of the recipient reader. Under no circumstances will any legal responsibility or blame be held against the publisher for any reparation, damages, or monetary loss due to the information herein, either directly or indirectly.

Respective authors own all copyrights not held by the publisher.

The information herein is offered for informational purposes solely, and is universal as so. The presentation of the information is without contract or any type of guarantee assurance.

The trademarks that are used are without any consent, and the publication of the trademark is without permission or backing by the trademark owner. All trademarks and brands within this book are for clarifying purposes only and are the owned by the owners themselves, not affiliated with this document.

Table Of Contents

CHAPTER 1 : WHAT IS PROCRASTINATION	1
QUOTES ABOUT PROCRASTINATION	34
CHAPTER 2 : WHY DO PEOPLE PROCRASTINATE?	37
CHAPTER 3 : THE MEAT OF THINGS 36 WAYS PROVEN	58
CHAPTER 4 : WHEN IS PROCRASTINATION GOOD?	109
CHAPTER 5 FAQ TO HALT PROCRASTINATION	124
CHAPTER 6 : CONCLUSION	141

Prologue

Jim is a New Yorker who has spent the bulk of his life living downtown New York. He finished college 3 years ago but has struggled to gain admission to college. His SATs have been terribly poor, and one wonders what has really happened. A few years ago, he wasn't exactly like this. A brilliant chap who understood calculus as early as 10, He had the best score in the regional Queen's Project Aptitude test by 12. He was destined for greatness given all the feats he had achieved at such an early age.

When he tried writing entrance examinations, he was never prepared. He always waited till it was almost deadline before making moves to study. Since there were new additions every year, he had to update his collection of books and knowledge. However, he had to wait till last minute before doing so. This wasn't enough time to cover for everything done. He was a chronic procrastinator. He always waited till the last minute before doing anything. This always spelled doom for him.

Do you see any of Jim in any of your friends, family or just perhaps maybe even yourself? I know. It is sometimes tough to acknowledge that we procrastinate and delay things which we ought to have done like eons ago, and it is no mean feat to cope with a colleague or loved one who does that consistently too! So it doesn't matter if you are getting this book for yourself or others, the main thing here is, what you will find in this book would be the tried and tested, proven solutions with which you can use to combat and rid yourself of the most debilitating effects that procrastination brings!

Get ready to be boosting your productivity and bringing about daily doses of self discipline which will see you clear through all those hateful tasks and then some, all without the shadow of procrastination lurking in the background. It shall be banished!

Of course, this whole gamut of productivity and anti procrastination techniques aren't going to be very much useful if anyone who reads it actually Procrastinates on taking definitive action isn't? It becomes a literal situation of all talk and no action which definitely would not serve us well at all. So, it is important for you to know that within the confines of this book, you will be getting two of the most powerful methods with which to halt and stop procrastination perpetually in its tracks. I kid you not. I am so excited about sharing this with you that I am just seriously tempted to write it all down here, but no no, it is not going to be beneficial to you just to hear it like this. These two secrets need to be coupled with some degree of thinking and self reflection to really unleash its usefulness.

I am really delighted and excited that we will be walking this journey of learning and sharing together, and more importantly to be able to bring about positive change in any lives which utilize the valuable knowledge that is contained within this book.

Remember, the purpose of this is to give anyone the tools to fix that procrastination habit and bring about increased productivity to work and life. Daily training and habitual usage of the tips contained therein will definitely aid in creating letting anyone see results much much quicker.

The excellence of life has always been a product of smart and hard work, consistently applied at the right areas, and with the proper guidance. This book will be your proper guidance. You will need to apply it consistently in the right areas. Together, you can achieve all that you want and more!

CHAPTER 1 :
WHAT IS PROCRASTINATION

Never postpone for tomorrow or the day after tomorrow what you can do today; barns are not filled by those who postpone and aimlessly waste time. Work prospers with care; those who postpone battle with ruin.

It is not uncommon to see many people take procrastination for laziness. It is often referred to as an abominable flaw. However, this is a very wrong notion that has to be refuted. Procrastination is the act of postponing the execution of an action or an activity. Such actions are carried out at the last minute or when it is a little too late. More often than not, such executions are below par and unacceptable. Laziness refers to the unwillingness to do work or put efforts in a particular action. There is no inclination to do any activity. This shows that both subjects are quite different. Someone who procrastinates might be inclined to do work but shall postpone the execution to a later date. Often, such a person can engage in frivolous or less important activities instead of concentrating on the task at hand. In the case of Jim, his PS4 console is laden with various games ranging from FIFA 18, Call of Duty: Modern Warfare, Modern Combat 5, Grand Theft Auto V to Assassins Creed. He invites his friends over on a daily basis, and they play multiplayer mode, or he connects to the Internet to play against other internet users. If he doesn't want to play games, he is glued to his laptop to keep himself up to date with Madam Secretary, Suits, House of Cards and the like.

This example shows that procrastination is intentional, pre-planned and not accidental. It can become a habit that might not be realized on time until it has gone so deep it can't be stopped in an instant. Also, if someone undertakes a project and is unable to complete the project due to the undue and needless postponement, this is procrastination.

What is procrastination?

Giving a holistic view, Procrastination is gotten from a Latin origin *procrastinus* which is a past participle of *procrastinare*, which when broken, means a *pro* (forward) and *crastinus* (from tomorrow). When putting together, the word procrastination is given a full picture, and clear direction is fully provided.

Procrastination is the act of engaging in actually less pressing tasks instead of the more pressing ones or carrying out trivial tasks in place of the more important tasks. That moment you find yourself trying very hard to do the required thing at the moment that you should or would like to do, procrastination has set indefinitely. Having said so, procrastination is also engaging in the more pleasurable things than engaging in, the less pleasurable activities, and postponing and putting off waiting tasks to another chosen time. To classify a particular behavior as procrastination oriented, certain attributes are present in such behavior. They are unproductive, time wasting, unnecessary and delaying.

Constantly, procrastination is voluntarily delaying a planned course of action despite expecting the worst of doing the wrong thing that moment. Therefore when you see yourself taking on trivial tasks with a long history of putting things off instead of performing the meaningful tasks, you have started procrastinating. Notably, it is safe to say that procrastination is the bridge between intention and taken action.

How Procrastination Can Hurt You in Business and Relationships

Procrastination showing its weight can go ahead to affect an individual negatively in business and relationships by acting as a barrier from living life to the fullest. More recent research studies have gone to show that people regret more for the things they haven't done than the things they have done. The feelings of regret more often tend to stay with people much longer. The result of procrastination is a result of wasting time that could be invested into something much more meaningful or a task that requires that it attention or completion. When the enemy in the form of procrastination is conquered, you will be able to achieve more, while in so doing your business and relationship life will be improved; thus enjoying the potential that they both have to offer. Having said so, it is also important for you to know that your self-confidence is also a crucial part of your success in both your relationship and business life.

It is even more important for those in leadership as procrastination may influence employees and colleagues to feel that you are delaying progress. Another mistake we make is not recognizing the procrastination habit and its complexities; we do not consider it a habit and believe we are just doing it for now because we have a lot on our plate. It encroaches on other aspects of our lives that we even postpone the minutest of tasks because we believe there will always be time. You need to take action on a task — even when you're not in the mood to do it. Naturally, you will not always be in the mood to perform tasks or responsibilities, but the ability to motivate ourselves into doing them is the difference between a lazy procrastinator and a hardworking person. Properly plan your life in such a way that you won't be heavily reliant on your to-do list. Quickly complete daily tasks using a simple time-management technique. It is quite easy to cultivate the habit of procrastination, but it takes a more disciplined and determined effort to say no to procrastinating. You just need to cultivate the same habits used by several successful people such as Eric Schmidt (Executive Chairman, Alphabet Inc.), Steve Jobs (CEO and co-founder of Apple Inc.), Jeffrey Bezos (founder, chairman, and CEO of Amazon), Brett David (29-year-old CEO of Prestige Imports Motor Group Miami) and adapt them as part of your routine. While these successful people also experience identical fears and limitations as you, they have been able to take consistent action due to personal training and discipline. To quit procrastinating has to do with training the mind to always stick to its plans, to undertake its due tasks at their set time, to say no to anxiety caused by stress, fear and a sense of incompetence. Identify the important things in your life, so you won't have any qualms ignoring everything else. Decline pointless tasks without upsetting your friends, loved ones or boss. In our daily lives, we will receive invaluable tasks which may be compulsory or not and tasks which are the direct opposite of invaluable - cheap; it boils down to you to decide which is pointless and which is important to accept as a task. This reduces the amount of stress you will go through as a result of tasks and gives you ample time to do them before their appointed time is up.

WHAT DO PEOPLE PROCRASTINATE ABOUT?

There is nothing in life that cannot be procrastinated really. People procrastinate about going for a medical check-up while they are fit even though they are meant to undergo such process once in three months. When they fall sick, they do not have any choice than to seek the medical attention they ought to have sought as a preventive means. In the case of Jim, he procrastinates about his education. He does not do the required study when necessary. He waits till the 'dying minute' before he acts. He never covers the number of books he ought to.

The most obvious areas that are affected by procrastination include but not limited to study, work, etc. while the less obvious are health, food, exercise, relationships, etc. The fact is any project we want to undertake or any task we want to be pursued can be affected by procrastination. Individuals set certain goals, aims or objectives that need to be met or achieved. Such can be viable sources of procrastination. Everyone procrastinates in different measures. Some can keep on top of a situation while others wallow in the procrastination pool.

At one point in our lives, we are required to assess what facets of our lives suffer from procrastination. We need to create a chart and think about the moments we have procrastinated. What were they related to? What were the tasks? What were the deadlines? Did we meet them? Those are questions that shall provide answers to our various problems. Information gathering is quite important to ascertain specific problems.

What is this book going to teach you and how it is going to be structured?

Types Of Procrastinators

- *The Perfectionist:* People who belong to this category are disturbed by the thought of not meeting expectations. They think of every possible outcome, and they think that they might be a massive flop. They strive so hard but do not meet up to standard. Sometimes, they do not even start because they have decided the outcome themselves. An illustration is given of a soccer player who is signed by one of the world's biggest clubs (e.g., Manchester United) from a relatively low club like Hellas Verona. He is placed on the bench and on Matchday 1, he watches Paul Pogba dazzle in the midfield making somber runs and doing flicks and tricks that help the team secure a massive 3 points win. Pogba is the player's rival and having watched him that day; he thinks he cannot measure up to him. Therefore, he strives so hard to gain his manager's confidence in the training ground. Unfortunately, he has the weight of the world on him, and he thinks he is not performing up to expectations. He is shorn of confidence by his thoughts and gives up too easily.

- *The Dreamer:* A lot of people suffer from this kind of procrastination. Many people are so great at planning actions in their head. They envision an almost flawless execution of plans. They think of the potential hindrances or stumbling blocks that can come their way. They think of ways to counter such occurrences. However, the greatest hindrance they face is doing the actual work. They feel stressed sitting down to go through a task for a given time especially if it is a mental one. They tend to postpone taking actions till the 'convenient' time. Writing could be seen as one such activity. Thinking about putting pen to paper and letting those linguistic phrases pour out in easy verses will appear much easier to do in the head than when actually doing it for such folks.
- *The Worrier:* Many people tend to worry about the negative parts of undertaking a project. They are pessimists who are based on 'what ifs.' They query the feasibility of a task. They think there is a chance it might not be successful neglecting the chance of being successful. They shy away from making decisions and do not like to delve into untested waters.
- *The Crisis Maker:* Those who belong to this category practically act when it is the last minute. This is the category Jim belongs to. They do not act until the 11th hour. Their favorite phrase

is "We work best under pressure." They like to wait until the deadline is approaching before they make any move.

- *The Defier:* These kinds of people are always defiant. They are aware of certain deadlines but do not care a hoot about it. Living up to expectations is not their primary concern. They just want to live life as it comes without having to worry about goals or objectives. They shy away from taking responsibilities for whatever situation they find themselves and the kind of choices they make.
- *The Overdoer:* These people load themselves with too much responsibility and more often than not, they fail to complete various tasks assigned to them. They lack the initiative to say no to certain requests. They have too much on their plate, and they cannot 'consume' all. They never have sufficient time to complete the various tasks at hand. On top of that, they like to make people happy thereby neglecting their emotional state.

This Book Will Teach You How People Develop Procrastination

"Procrastination is the thief of time." It is usually developed when people fear or dread, or have anxiety about, the important task awaiting them. Procrastination is an automatic, negative, problem habit of needlessly postponing and delaying a timely and relevant activity until another day or time. It always involves a negative emotion that ranges from a whisper of affect to panic. The process always includes a diversionary activity. It practically always involves procrastination thinking, such as "I'll fix the problem later." This complex, automatic, problem habit typically coexists with other negative states, such as anxiety, depression, impulse control challenges, organizational challenges, distractibility, substance abuse, self-doubts, perfectionism, indecisiveness, and other. When procrastination co-occurs with other conditions, it is a complex form of procrastination. To eliminate this negative feeling, people procrastinate preferring to play a video game or check Pinterest. That brings about a better feeling temporarily, but unfortunately, reality stares at them in the end. Procrastinating involves waiting and delaying, avoiding and languishing over tasks and responsibilities. It is a self-defeating behavior and can have lasting effects on our lives. Procrastinators waste tremendous amounts of time. The pleasure principle has a vital role to play in procrastination; one may desire to evade negative emotions and to defer stressful tasks. As the time limit for the task you procrastinate draws closer, the stress starts getting to you, and you may eventually procrastinate more to avoid this stress. Procrastination is not a decisive action; it is not a one-time decision but a continuous decision to put aside important tasks and responsibilities because of feelings of anxiety, incapability, fear and mostly the envisioned stress we think it'll bring. It's quite easy to find excuses for not starting or completing a task. We just find the time to eat the tub of ice cream, play that game, but just not do the task that is silently awaiting us.

You need to find a balance between finding a valid reason to procrastinate and finding a creative way to avoid taking action. Most of our feelings of procrastination arise from self-limiting beliefs or a subconscious fear. By taking your time to explore these thoughts, you'll realize it's easy to overcome them and build a mindset that is action-oriented.

Your mind is an incredible machine that enables you to create anything from your imagination. It could, however, limit your ability to get things done if not properly monitored. At times we get stuck with a project not because we lack the desire to do so but because of maladaptive thought patterns that spring up in our heads.

The root cause of why people procrastinate comes from our low self-confidence. When these thoughts are not promptly checked they lead to you making "excuses" for why a task or project can't be completed. However, when these excuses are challenged, you'll realize that most arise as a result of hidden fears or destructive habit patterns.

The first word we utter most times we procrastinate is that "It doesn't matter." People often avoid tasks which seem unimportant. Sometimes it's not time-critical while at times it's an unpleasant task that is unrelated to a long-term goal.

No matter what your thoughts are, there are times when we defer a task because it doesn't seem to be important. Of course, most tasks or responsibilities are placed on a priority scale, and we decide which comes before which and which should be done before which. However, tasks, which we consider minute or too simple, may be postponed even if there is no other task on our plate because we consider it simple. It, however, becomes complicated when there is pressure attached to it as a result of postponing it to the last minute. Making simple decision making a habit will help you overcome the "It doesn't matter" excuse.

You either get busy with completing a task or be bold enough to get rid of it. As you'll learn, one of the effective ways to get rid of procrastination excuses is to make tough life decisions—even if that means getting rid of things that once seemed important. It is either you will do it at that time, or you decide that you will not do it and get it assigned to someone else. But, for tasks which are official, handed to you and are compulsory, the best solution is to do them at their appointed time.

Another way we develop procrastination is when we say "I feel overwhelmed and have too much to do."

We all experience overwhelming moments which seems like our to-do lists never gets exhausted no matter how hard we work. This problem usually affects those who have the "Superman mentality" where they feel responsible personally accomplish tasks on their own. Concentrating on essential projects and delegating or eliminating the rest can remove feelings of being overwhelmed.

Once you understand how to identify the important things you'll realize that it's easy to handle each task single-handedly and consistently accomplish things. Another valid excuse those who procrastinate often give is "I don't have time right now." Sometimes you may be engrossed in a certain project, and it doesn't make sense to commence another one. However, the excuse of having no time often leads to a disgusting procrastination habit where you always defer undertaking important things.

Saying there is not enough time seems to give empty promise of a perfect future when work will be easier, and you will have more time to work.

In some peoples subconscious mind, they just hope that the need to do the task will eventually disappear. By delaying action until that imaginary "someday," there is a high likelihood that you'll never undertake this project. By thinking of this task, what negative thought pops into your head? Find a solution to that thought by countering it with the truth. For instance, thinking "I'll never be able to do this," you might say to yourself, "If others can do it, I can also do same." The task has been thought about, dealt with what's holding you back, and your destructive thinking fixed. Now, break down the big job into a series of little actionable steps, so you focus solely on handling the next little task. Delve into the nitty-gritty for each project, including little details like whom you will talk with, where and when you'll be working, and duration for each step. (This will stop you from getting overwhelmed as each step is actionable).

Nobody is above making procrastination excuses. No matter how successful you have been, you will sometimes experience a reason not to take action on a project. That's why one needs to form habits that specifically prevent the excuses leads to procrastination. Once you know the reason for developing the habit of procrastination, it makes it easy to proceed to the next step. Low self-confidence, low self-esteem and lack of self-compassion are feelings that develop the habit of procrastination. Low self-esteem or confidence will ultimately affect every aspect of your life, even your daily tasks. It hinders the ability to be creative; reduces or even eliminates the conviction that you can surpass difficult tasks and situations. But in the long run procrastinating will begin to affect job performance. The mood and state of mind will also be affected as worry, fear, or stress sets in. Psychologists accept that procrastination is an emotional reaction. One of the three core emotions always drive it. For example, it may be fear that's driving your inability to get the job done thoroughly and on time. Another is anger; maybe because you have to do something you hate or resent? Or may it is sadness because you feel inadequate or not fit to handle the task. Study yourself and try to identify the emotions responsible for why you procrastinate. Fear, anger, and sadness are just pure sensations that get stuck in the bodies. If they're bottled up and not allowed to gain expression, they will build up inside us like a pressure cooker. Privately, do exaggerated shivering to get rid of fear; punch a pillow or throw your fist in the air to release anger; or watch an emotional movie that makes you shed tears to get rid of sadness. It may sound silly, but it works.

What about Procrastination and Depression

There is nothing wrong about postponing completion of a task in order to allocate enough time to do it properly. But, putting things off impulsively is a different story. Procrastination and depression go hand in hand just like obesity and diabetes. Depression is a factor that causes procrastination and the most time comes before it. However, depression can also come after a series of continuous procrastination which may seem to choke you up, leaving you anxious and afraid of their impending due time. The common symptoms such as fatigue and ineptness, make it easy to say, "I'll just postpone this till tomorrow when I feel better." Within a twinkle of the eye that deadline has dawned on us, and we have started panicking. How best can we deal with this panic? Bury your head in the sand like the vulture and hope it goes away! No, that won't do, although one can easily fall into the trap of procrastination and as the panic increases, so does the depression.

The more depressed we become depressed, the more reality we avoid. Procrastination is a form of avoidance thereby one can view it as a coping strategy albeit one that comes with negative effects. We all develop our coping strategy for difficult situations over time, but we may be faced with varying situations to cope with. Procrastination is developed from a lack of experience, inability to manage time effectively, lack of interest, underestimating the difficulty level of the task, pain aversion, and fear of failure. While evading decisions or actions has the potential of offering short-term succor, over time the effects can be psychologically harmful. Other negative, coping strategies include drug abuse, alcohol, and even overworking. Most depressed people find it difficult to be productive. Most work such as paid employment, babysitting and housekeeping is a chore to the depressed. It exhausts us, leaves us feeling worse than before, physically and emotionally worn out, instead of us to be energized and proud of ourselves. Other depressed people seem to work very hard all the time, but, they achieve little a reward for their efforts. Procrastination and depression have a strong connection to each other and inaction can make you feel that your life is falling apart. This feeling makes hope disappears while you have a generally negative view of life. It's a negative cycle, the less action taken to remedy things, the more depressed you become. Various reasons abound why you might experience procrastination, but it yields the same result: a feeling of, helplessness and being unable to find a solution to things. Depression is quite different from feeling sad. While sadness simply means being unhappy for a short time, depression goes beyond that. In depression you don't only feel sad, you also have the feeling of hopelessness in things getting better.

Once this feeling persists, you will find it very difficult to take action, and that's where procrastination sets in. According to doctors definition and explanation of depression and sadness, it observed that depression is an intense feeling of unhappiness that goes on for weeks, months or years in some cases. One damaging effect of depression is that it can negatively impact your day to day activity and the way you feel generally. Procrastination may be an indication of hopelessness and lack of motivation which may also come from your depressive state.

I'm of the view that they are both connected and that inactivity can make you feel that your life is stagnant. This feeling brings about a lack of hope and a generally negative perception of life. There are several reasons why you might experience procrastination, but the result stays the same: a feeling of inability to effect a change and helplessness.

However, it's certain that depression worsens procrastination and when you realize that you are procrastinating, and you refuse to take action at the appropriate time, you feel worse, and your depression worsens. The first question is: "Does depression lead to procrastination or is it the other way round?" No, depression doesn't lead to procrastination, but it can make it worse. However, frequent procrastination without taking action when you know you should lead to depression. There is nothing as motivating as you taking steps towards achieving your goal, but depression or lack of motivation can inhibit you from taking any step, and that will surely, make you feel even more negative. Data was collated from undergraduates with the use of a self-report measure, and an interesting finding was made. As expected, she found a significantly positive correlation between depression and procrastination. This positive correlation shows that the more depressed we are, the more we tend towards procrastination, and vice versa. This is expected because depression comes with the inability to finish tasks. The person tries to shy away from activities that will cause anxiety, distress or discomfort. Ironically, the act of evading the activity doesn't make it leave, so tensions are heightened because of this avoidance. It is like an emotional weakness which corrupts every other aspect of our lives, hindering us from performing simple tasks or daily routines. And since we feel a kind of emotional weakness in performing them, we tend to postpone them till a date when we hope we'll feel better which, is under probability. When you feel depressed, you suffer from a painful down mood. You may withdraw from life, feel a profound sense of loneliness and worthlessness, and believe that life will continue in this way forever. Can you turn this bad situation around? You can if you don't procrastinate. Procrastination goes in two ways here; when in a bad situation we postpone tasks, shifting them to a further date. But, we also do not try to comprehend the reason(s) why we are in that bad situation, or we are depressed so we also postpone that thinking the situation will dissolve all by itself. Sometimes it does, and most times it doesn't. It is either we forgo the unpalatable situations surrounding us and focus on performing our tasks to avoid procrastination, or we try to source out the reason for that unpalatable situation, putting an end to it and moving on to completing our tasks.

In both procrastination and depression, you may avoid taking corrective action. For example, if you feel lethargic, you may believe you don't have the energy to take corrective actions. This pessimism is a catalyst for procrastination. Believe you are helpless to overcome a depressed mood and reconnect with other people, and you've given yourself an excuse to procrastinate. When this secondary procrastination follows depression, you'd better learn to get past this barrier. One easy way to fail is to disbelieve your capability. The inability to overlook temporary weaknesses that will fade out once the task is being performed will hinder you from performing it. It takes a never say die attitude to keep being strong in the face of depressing situations.

To the barest minimum- our phones, it is very evident that a depressed person may not even pick up the phone to entertain or amuse him or herself even if he or she is a phone addict. Depression comes with a general distaste for everything; even the liked and more for the unliked. So when you are depressed, and there are dishes all over the counter, it is not because you are lazy. It is because you don't have the energy to motivate yourself. Telling yourself words like "Never mind move my body off the couch," even if I feel worse by mere seeing the dishes. So the dishes accumulate and the more they do, the worse I feel. You are failing the first step of housekeeping. When you are well, you find it easy to make decisions and keep them in a positive perspective that if I can do this now, I can do it again. When you are depressed, you cannot manage that optimism in such a healthy way, which is bad enough, but even worse is the shame that goes with it. It's the loss of an ability that you depend on, and you are used to having. The notion that what you did before you can't do again is shattered because of the feeling of depression, making you postpone that task that you have performed before.

Depressed people procrastinate a lot. Procrastination means putting off what you "should" do now for a later time. The word "should" may arise from without, as with the student who delays over the assignment, or from within, like you planting your garden. When it comes from without, it's easy to notice the change that procrastination brings. When it comes from within, it becomes difficult to notice that procrastination comes from depression immediately. Procrastinators perception and assumptions about work are so false. They assume that those who are productive are always in a positive and energetic such that they easily jump right to work and quickly do what needs to be done.

Contrary to this belief, motivation comes after action instead of the other way around. When we compel ourselves to face the task at hand, we realize it isn't as bad as we think, and we start to feel good about the progress we are making. Work proceeds the positive frame of mind. Closely related to this mix-up about motivation is the thought that things should come easy. Depressed people believe that those who perform excellently well at work always feel confident and attain their goals easily; because they don't feel this way, they play down their chances of success. But again, most successful people are of the belief that they will experience hard times, frustrations, and setbacks along the way. Knowing this beforehand will not make them get thrown off their game and descend into self-blame whenever they encounter a problem. If we decide to wait until we feel prepared and fired up, we'll spend a lot of our lives waiting for an opportunity that won't come.

On the other hand, procrastination can help protect the self-esteem of the depressed. You can make positive confessions like "I would have done it better if you I been able to do it." Procrastination also results from the depressed person's tendency to be a perfectionist which is a serious problem. Research has it that the harder a depressed person tries to be perfect, the worse his chances of recovery. Striving to achieve perfection with every single little piece of a project exposes us to disappointment and frustration. There is a connection between the way a procrastinator thinks and mild to serious depression in many people. For some, procrastination leads to depression (reactive depression) as a personality trait, while for others, innate depression causes procrastination due to their illness.

Consequently, procrastination can cause depression and depression can lead to procrastination. Depression arises when one is withdrawn from the normal psychological activity. Depressed people perform less interaction with the society than they did when they were thinking and behaving healthily. Depressed people are detached from people because they may find human interaction too stressful and they live in fear of disappointment. If you experience innate depression, you will also experience low motivation. This triggers a chain reaction where one leads to the other. This implies that you procrastinate about making serious life decisions and even feel incompetent and nervous about making decisions. The lack of motivation ensures you to start a task only to stop mid-way. Part of that behavior is looking for several excuses not to make decisions and perform the needed tasks.

Awareness is the first step in overcoming procrastination. It means figuring out your thoughts and habits. If you're going through a moment of depression, this can be challenging, and it may do you much favor to consult a therapist who will help you pull out of depression. It is possible that you've been procrastinating because you face a daunting decision or tasks ahead of you. You need to break these task into small, realistic and achievable goals. Try to avoid situations that encourage easy distractions or that disrupt your positive mindset or productivity. For example, if you need to study try to find an appropriate environment, away from friends and noise. Break off habits that could warrant distraction.

An example might be a teacher listening to great music alongside marking of papers. Instead, the music should be used as a reward for accomplishing the task. Recognize that depression has correctable features. For example, if you believe you are helpless to change, find exceptions to that line of depressive thinking. You can take that corrective action. Depression normally feels debilitating. Nevertheless, you can act, even in small measure, to progressively master techniques to end your depression.

It will show you that Defeating Procrastination starts from an idea

What is an idea? It is the seed of every civilization that has been built.

The Mesopotamian civilization became great in their ideas, architectural structures, and code of laws because numerous men within the civilization held ideas. The ancient Pharaohs of Egypt had ideas, and these were the driving force that enables them to embark upon the construction of the great edifices that continue to blow our minds at the present day. An idea was the driving force that enabled movie directors like Stan Lee to begin a revolutionary process within Hollywood. In the same vein, the entire Marvel franchise which includes comics, movies of superheroes like Thor, Captain America, Black Panther, etc. as well as the DC universe which includes the Franchise of Superman, Wonder woman, etc., were all driven by a single idea. The freedom of the United States of America from the rulership of Britain started as an idea that continued to be spread among the founding fathers of the nation such as Jefferson, etc. The turn of the World War 2 in favor of the Allied powers that included France, Britain, Russia and the United States, began as an idea in the mind of seasoned statesmen like Winston Churchill as well as Josef Stalin and Theodore Roosevelt. The fall of the Soviet Union in the 1990s started as an idea in the mind of a revolutionary mind of Mikhail Gorbachev who was the ruling Premier of Russia at the time. The creation of the Eragon franchise by Christopher Paollini, Kingkiller Chronicles by Patrick Rothfuss, Harry Potter Franchise by JK Rowling, Percy Jackson and the Olympian franchise by Rick Riodan as well as other book franchises all started with singular ideas. The super-fast Boeing passenger and cargo planes began as a result of an idea. Ford, Ferrari, Mercedes and a host of other companies began as a result of nagging ideas. These ideas were held in an esteemed way within the minds of the people who got them, and one binding factor that is noticeable within all of them is that they were careful not to become the ones that procrastinate. This is because they held fast to the

In the business world, the first lesson that you get to learn is that everything you do begins from your mind. Even as the book begins to delve deep into the particular topic of procrastination, you should be able to adopt the open mindset that would enable the lessons within to sink deeply into your subconscious mind. No one on earth can afford to remain like a granite rock that is impervious to any element: rather, we should all strive to have an open mind that would enable us to internalize lessons that we are being taught on a regular basis.

It will show you that Procrastination can be very deadly

Procrastination can lead to one's death as I have seen and heard of people who died from it. "It can be something like noticing a lump in your breast and keeping silent about it and leaving it untreated." An unnecessarily delayed medical visit can definitely lead to something more dangerous.

Ignoring the fact that procrastination exists and not paying attention to its causes can significantly impact one's life in general. Procrastination tends to be a more serious problem when it affects every aspect of one's life. There are countless causes of procrastination one of it is depression which comes with symptoms such as hopelessness, helplessness and a lack of energy. When procrastination becomes full-fledged, it translates into a personality trait, at this stage its called chronic procrastination. At this stage, procrastination has become a habitual self-destructive pattern. It has now become a habit to put tasks off impulsively.

The chronic procrastinator cannot undertake any task on time which will eventually result in serious career struggles, recurring financial problems, and reduced quality of life. Chronic procrastination may lead to disability psychological and dysfunction in several aspects of life and may bring about low self-esteem and a persistent sense of shame.

Many individuals considered as "chronic procrastinators" are in reality suffering from an associated mental health problem like depression or Attention Deficit Disorder (ADD). These individuals often find it difficult to understand why they struggle to "get it together," and can eventually settle for a life of frustration, struggle, and underachievement. Unfortunately, this is caused by their limited knowledge about what procrastination is about. Even amongst mental health professionals, some only view procrastination as a "bad habit." How many of us avoid seeing their doctor or dentist only for us to realize that the delay has brought about more complications? The health implications of depressed procrastination vary, but according to research, it shows that they can lead to higher risk.

It will teach you about the Chronic Procrastination and the Time Management Problem

Procrastination is the act of deferring or delaying a task. It's the avoidance of doing a task that needs to be accomplished at present, more or less postponing a task until its deadline. Procrastination becomes chronic when little things which do not take any effort to do are postponed; it may be regarded as a very high level of laziness. Procrastination can affect any aspect of life such as putting off house cleaning, seeing a dentist for that toothache, submitting a job report or business proposal. Procrastination can cause feelings of guilt, depression, self-doubt, and inadequacy. To procrastinate can hinder productivity. Most times we as human beings tend to postpone our tasks and responsibilities until the last minute, practically because of the notion that there will always be time. We fail to understand that time is a measurement of periods; there is always a specific and limited period for everything. From the time a task or responsibility is given, the duration for that task begins to countdown. We often forget that time doesn't wait for anyone and continue to postpone our responsibilities till they reach their expected time. We, however, make it a habit that we not only do it for one task or responsibility but for several, and in their due time, we have multiple tasks choking us up which we have postponed over and over again.

Most times, when we procrastinate, we end up worse off for it. Whether academically or socially, procrastinating leads to a lot of tasks being on your plate with more than half of the allotted time to be used to do them gone. Everyone procrastinates things until the last minute at some point or the other, but procrastinators are chronically used to avoiding difficult tasks and are always on the lookout for distractions. Some people are of the view that they suddenly become highly productive when they procrastinate! Instead of filling the tax form, they choose to clean the whole house, even though they do hate to clean. While others try to forget about the urgent task by doing something fun instead. While it might seem harmless pushing tasks to one side with the intention of doing it later, it can have negative ripple effects. Procrastination at large shows our perennial struggle with self-control and inability to tell yourself that you need to do what you need to do now! It depends partially on our state of mind, as well as our inability to predict accurately how we'll feel the next day. "I don't feel like it" is prioritized over goals; however, it then sets in motion a downward spiral of negative emotions that prevent future effort. We forgo our goals because of a temporary, unrealized feeling of laziness or weakness that seems to override every other feeling of responsibility. We tend to view our tasks and responsibilities as stressful, no matter how minute they seem to be and ignoring them which is the same as procrastinating just brings more stress on us. It's like a cycle of ignoring our tasks because they look or seem stressful which results in more stress and our bid to continue to ignore this leads us not to realize that the feeling of stress will never end until we complete these tasks.

When we procrastinate the temporary feeling of ease has no foundation and is easily shattered by the feeling that there will come a due time for these tasks. So there is more or less no rest for a person that procrastinates since it'll always be at the back of his/ her mind that there is a task waiting for you which will not go away, is compulsory and has a limited time. The unrelenting feeling of stress leads to fatigue which will eventually lead to both physical and mental exhaustion. Exhaustion will also not allow you to perform in other aspects of your daily life; it will deter you from performing to your full extent in other spheres which will affect your creativity. Procrastination was revealed to be higher on tasks perceived as unpleasant or imposed than on tasks which people believed they lacked the required skills for accomplishing the task. Once a task seems big or greater than we presume we can handle we become anxious. Humans generally tend to shy away from things that make us uncomfortable or move away from our comfort zone. If a task is going to make a person uncomfortable most times, we do everything to avoid it, passing it onto the next person and the next person does the same until he or she has no one to pass it on to. Nevertheless, financial incentives can spur a person not to procrastinate. But, a person who takes on tasks, which he or she is incapable of executing because of the monetary incentive attached to them, will probably procrastinate in the end due to the number of responsibilities he has taken on his plate.

It is evident that a bulk of the world's population delay tasks. However, researches done over the years have indicated that a frightening percentage of people are chronic procrastinators. This category of people does not do tasks frequently. Rather, they tend to delay the execution of tasks. They are of the opinion that time management cannot be effective due to certain situations. They do not think of time management as the ideal thing to worry about. As long as they can meet deadlines, they do not have to worry about any other thing. They tend to make an excuse for every failure or shortcoming.

Chronic procrastination can be defined as an irrelevant, nonsensical delay or a very important project or task. It also refers to postponing the execution of tasks or projects until the last minute. It is important these delays are done so frequently. This confirms the reason why they are called chronic procrastinators.

Different features characterize chronic procrastinators. They include, but not limited to, low level of self-confidence, social and emotional anxiety.

Various researches conducted has revealed that various people who exhibit chronic procrastination, engage in self-destructive behaviors which include frequent excuse making, non-review of performance, shifting blame on others apart from them. Many have been thought as reasons why people procrastinate, but the chief causative agent is fear of failure has been identified as the principal causative agent. It is not uncommon to hear procrastinators say that they do not have enough time to start or finish given tasks or projects. However, if a non-procrastinator is given the same amount of time to complete a task, he or she shall do so with ample time left.

Chronic procrastinators may say they perform better under pressure, but more often than not that's their way of justifying putting things off. The result of working under pressure can never equal that which is done when you are ease; it far outweighs that which is done when you are choked up with tasks. We have all faced procrastination at one point or another. For as long as we are humans, we have always struggled with delays and procrastinating on issues that concern us. To procrastinate can hinder productivity. Due to the number of tasks postponed, fatigue and stress will set in thinking about their deadline. They act as deterrents to creativity, as a mentally tired person will not look to further stress his brain in ruminating on an issue to bring results. During our moments of productivity when we figure out momentarily on how to stop procrastinating, we feel satisfied and accomplished.

The positive side? Overcoming procrastination is possible and realistic albeit with effort. Most perfectionists are also procrastinators; it is psychologically permissive never to undertake a task than to face the possibility of failing. Putting off a task is not procrastination as long as there are rational reasons for doing so. The rational reasons justify this act, which forms a reasonable excuse to postpone the tasks. Since there is a reasonable excuse that will be proffered there should be no stress in postponing the task. It, however, does not mean the tasks or responsibilities will leave the mind, but they are however put aside for several reasons and obviously for a greater purpose or task.

Chronic procrastination is as a result of feelings that the task seems large, complex, and too overwhelming. When a task is more than the person's ability, or when it is exaggerated in the mind of the person procrastination sets in. It may also be that the task looks tedious and boring and the person feels it may dim his or her creative spark. Not knowing how the task is done makes it difficult to start and some people view it as hard to get motivated until things become urgent and a deadline is close. Negative thoughts and feelings also get in the way of doing the task, which may not serve as reasonable excuses to postpone the task but deter you from performing them. A person that procrastinates must realize they have a problem and find effective ways to overcome procrastination because they are putting their health, family, and job at risk. It becomes a lifestyle when it becomes chronic. Some people don't view chronic procrastinating as a bad thing due to the common belief that they, "work best under pressure." However, the truth is that procrastinating can cause harm to one's life.

Chronic procrastination impacts Relationships. When a procrastinator works in a team, their inability to do the required task assigned to them can delay completion of projects. This will, in turn, affect the relationship the procrastinator has with the other members of the team. This may signal the end to such friendships and cause others to avoid working with the procrastinator on future projects. It is a fallacy to believe that people work better under pressure. Procrastors put unnecessary stress and pressure on themselves, which may cause them to be developmental and physical exertion.

Issues with Self-Regulation - procrastinators tend to develop excessive consumption of alcohol since they are dully stressed with all manner of tasks and responsibilities they are struggling to forget. Alcoholism provides a simple way to forget procrastinated tasks, but its results are very negatively exerting. Increased Health Issues will come the person's way since he or she is under great stress daily. Procrastinators tend to have their immune system compromised which predisposes them to colds and flu. Also, procrastinators have issues with insomnia as the tasks keep lingering in the thoughts hence inability to sleep. Procrastination affects people of all ages. People suffering from this habit don't hurt their academic or careers only, but they also create an unnecessary relationship and health problems.

If you or a close friend is a chronic procrastinator, some steps can be taken to change such behavior.

For a student experiencing chronic procrastination, it can be due to the Fear of Failure – Some people avoid working on school projects due to their fear of failure. They have the feeling that even with their best they will fail, so they get discouraged from doing the work. By abandoning things and not putting all their efforts into a project, the procrastinator is setting themselves up for failure. Another reason is the Fear of Success – This is the opposite of fear of failure, people who perform excellently on a project and achieve great things fear to be unable to repeat that success. They have the mindset that they may not be able to perform as well as, or better than, their previous accomplishment, so they resort to procrastinating. Some people also procrastinate due to the expectations placed on them by family and friends. If someone grows up in the family where the educational and career standard is high, such individual may delay doing class assignments, score less than average, and potentially fail the course, all as an act of rebellion.

Boredom and/or Lack of Motivation – When a subject seems boring to a student, such student might experience procrastination. Such a student finds it difficult to find motivation or inspiration. Such can lead to incomplete or poorly written assignments.

This Book will teach you ways to Stop Procrastination

There are various strategies we can make use of to stop procrastinating. Each concept will be outlined, explained with examples of strategy in action. The first step is to give an instant reward for taking action. If you can find ways to make instant rewards for making long-term choices, procrastination becomes easier to avoid. One great way to bringing future rewards into the present moment is to employ a strategy known as temptation bundling.

6 Tips to Get the Best From This Book

1. Read with an Open Mind
2. Practice daily
3. Have your jotter and pen with you
4. Share it with Friends and Family
5. Make ample Research to add to your knowledge
6. Understand that you have to apply the values inside into forceful action

The process of reading this book will prove to be a difficult task at most times for the reader who has not learned the value of being firm in his character, but it will prove to be an excellent first step for you

QUOTES ABOUT PROCRASTINATION

-------*"Things may come to those who wait, but only the things left by those who hustle."*– **Abraham Lincoln**

-------*"My advice is never to do tomorrow what you can do today. Procrastination is the thief of time."*– **Charles Dickens**

-------*"Never put off for tomorrow, what you can do today."*– **Thomas Jefferson**

--------*"Procrastination is the bad habit of putting off until the day after tomorrow what should have been done the day before yesterday."*– **Napoleon Hill**

--------*"The really happy people are those who have broken the chains of procrastination, those who find satisfaction in doing the job at hand. They're full of eagerness, zest, productivity. You can be, too."7*– **Norman Vincent Peale**

--------*"A year from now you may wish you had started today."*– **Karen Lamb**

--------*"Don't wait. The time will never be just right."*– **Napoleon Hill**

-------- *"You cannot escape the responsibility of tomorrow by evading it today."*– **Abraham Lincoln**

---------- *"One of the greatest labor-saving inventions of today is tomorrow."* – **Vincent T. Foss**

-------- *"The two rules of procrastination: 1) Do it today. 2) Tomorrow will be today tomorrow."* – **Author Unknown**

-------- *"What may be done at any time will be done at no time."* – **Scottish Proverb**

-------- *"Tomorrow is often the busiest day of the week."* – **Spanish Proverb**

-------- *"The best way to achieve something is to begin."* – **Author Unknown**

-------- *"I remember that I read somewhere about an organization called Procrastinators Anonymous. It seems they had existed for some years but never had the chance to hold a meeting."* – **Unknown**

-------- *"Procrastination is like masturbation. It feels good at first, but in the end, you realize that you are only screwing yourself."* – **Author unknown, possibly from Monty Python?**

-------- *"How soon not now, becomes never."* – **Martin Luther**

-------- *"In delay there lies no plenty."* – **William Shakespeare**

-------"Anyone can do any amount of work, provided it isn't the work he is supposed to be doing at that moment"– **Robert Benchley**

-------"Whatever you want to do, do it now! There are only so many tomorrows."– **Michael Landon**

CHAPTER 2 :
WHY DO PEOPLE PROCRASTINATE?

There are numerous reasons why people procrastinate. Most of these reasons always turn out to be valid or unnecessary reasons, but it all depends on whose perspective we see them. Take for example, if as an employee, you are given a task to carry out by your manager, and you decide to procrastinate because you do not have an idea of where to start or end. The reason behind your procrastination, of course, is valid to you at this point, but not to your manager whose job is to get you to perform the task. So the reasons for procrastination are highly dependent on a particular perspective. Although most times, perspectives tend to be a mutual thing, like you just procrastinated because you are just lazy. We will be discussing these reasons with no particular perspective in mind. When reading these reasons why people procrastinate, I want you to hold the torch of examination very close to yourself in order to easily spot out the reasons why you procrastinate. The reason for this is that human beings often make the unconscious effort to spot out challenges within other people without pausing to think that they may constitute part of the problem. As this book will begin to reel out the reasons, I can mentally picture you saying,

Yeah. That is how Mary my co-worker acts

True! Bob, my ex-husband, procrastinated due to these reasons.

Yes! My son does this all the time.

While it may probably be true that those people you just called are chronic offenders due to the reasons listed below, the aim of this chapter is to help you recognize the reasons why YOU, not Mary, Bob, or Dylan, continues to procrastinate because frankly, their reasons for procrastination may have simulated from your inability to make the first move. Like a cow chews its curd after eating, I want you to ruminate deeply on that while we dive into the reasons why we procrastinate.

Lack Of Definition Of Goals And Objectives

Why exactly are you doing that task? What are you going to achieve in doing it?

The lack of definite answers to the questions above is the bedrock of procrastination. Do you have a particular task that you have been procrastinating? Check it, you are either yet to define the goals and objective of that particular task, or you simply have forgotten about the goals and objectives you had set. Defining your goals and objectives means that failure to finish the task will bring about consequences. This makes it a two-way thing; one is such that we procrastinate because we have no idea why we are to do a particular task. The other is such that we haven't considered the consequences of not having to do that task. For example, at one certain point in time, when you realize that you add weight and then decide you will work out every morning for a whole month to shed the weight. In doing this, you will start to diet. The goal of your task will be to lose weight; the objective was to work out every morning by jogging and of course being on a diet. The consequence therefore of not achieving this task for most people is that they would add more weight and will end up being angry.

The Fear Of Failure

Naturally, failing is not the desired result. Procrastinators have the tendency to believe that trying hard and failing is worse than not trying at all. Procrastination, therefore, becomes a way to protect ourselves from the perceived failure that we dread so much. Failure can be either inability to finish a task or not getting expected results.

Usain Bolt will probably never turn up for training if he is so scared of failing.

Barrack Obama wouldn't have become the first black president US if he was scared of losing at the polls and therefore refuse to run for the presidency.

There wouldn't be Facebook today if Mark Zuckerberg was so scared of failing that he didn't take Facebook outside his dormitories

And I probably wouldn't have written this book if I was scared that it will fail.

Most times, the building blocks to our self-esteem are hinged on how much we have either succeeded or failed. Everyone has their particular reason as to why they fear failure. Using myself, for example, the number one reason why I fear failure is the fact that I don't want to disappoint my loved ones. Some people fear failure because of ego; others fear simply because they simply hate failing.

Irrespective of the drive, procrastination tends to be an easy way to avoid tasks that will likely bring us a failure. The fear of failure is a two-way factor. It can either motivate you to get a job done, or it can get you not to get a job done.

The Feeling Of Being Overwhelmed

When there are so many highly prioritized things to do, it leads to the feeling of being overwhelmed, and this can either slow us down, or it will lead us to do something entirely different from what we should have done. For example, the secretary to the manager of a company, who is told to prepare a report for a board meeting, at the same time, being given a task to prepare a contract-bidding document for the manager. Then she closes early so she will pick up her little child from school, and then gets a notification of an unread message from her friend on her WhatsApp, asking her to help her choose between two shoes she hopes to buy. Which task do you think she will do first?

My best bet is that she will do the one that will take lesser time, and it will be to reply to her friend's message. This is because it is easier than the other tasks, even though it is relatively unconnected to the tasks assigned to her office as a secretary, or the duty as a mother. The fact is that when there are too many seemingly important things to do, it becomes difficult to get our priorities right. This, in turn, leads to a poor decision on what to do and hence, procrastination comes to play.

The case of having to stop working into the midnight in order to be able to work out every morning is also a good example of being overwhelmed. I know the whole scenario doesn't look overwhelming, but I needed to stay awake late to get my projects done while doing this; I tend to take a whole lot of junks to keep me from sleeping. And then again, I needed to shed some weight by working out early in the morning, but I can't afford to go late to school. So I have to wake up early. To wake up early, I either have to sleep early or sleep for a shorter period of time; this will either affect my health or my work. Does it look overwhelming now?

Priorities

The part of the human brain that controls thoughts and action functions by protecting itself by tending to take our prioritized actions serious because not having them sorted out will like a threat to its sanity. Procrastination can arise as a result of our inability to prioritize tasks and actions in order of their importance. We unconsciously do things that we have given more importance to while postponing or not even doing the less important ones. The best-selling movies on motivation till date are rooted in the athletic world. This is because athletes are perfect examples of individuals that have their priorities set and ongoing for years. A young athlete that wants to represent his country in the Olympics knows that he has to train more than just any other athlete because he has to be his best. Usain Bolt, the fastest human alive today was once asked what his number one goal is at the starting line and he said it was to finish better than his previous record. He went further to say that the race is not run in the field but before the race; outside the tracks. Here is someone that has set a goal for himself and to achieve it, he has recognized that there are priorities and one of them is to train – before the race. Training cuts across so many disciplines. In the case of Bolt, having to train is the most important task for him. Hanging out with friends all-day or spending his day chatting on social media comes last. Still on the weight shedding experience, when some people finally get over the procrastination of the need to work out and to go on a diet, the next problem they encountered is, having to stop activities that will keep them late into the night, thereby impeding their desire to wake up early. In short, they discovered that staying late awake had a major influence in their intake of junks.

Denial

For procrastination to be identified as procrastination, it has to be with acceptance on the side of the individual. But what happens when we pretend that a particular act of procrastination is not actually what it is? Does it stop it from being procrastination? Well, no. Denial of procrastination itself is one major reason why people procrastinate, and this denial always comes with alternative excuses.

We convince ourselves that we are not procrastinating because we are doing something else. Sometimes we tend to be totally oblivious of the word 'procrastination' while all this is going on. For example, there was a time a friend had a rash skin reaction to a particular body lotion she was using. She knew she had to see a dermatologist immediately, but she kept on postponing her appointment. It didn't seem like procrastination at this time, because she was in actual denial as she gave silly excuses as to why she was yet to see a doctor. The excuses were so invalid that it got to the point that she thought this way, "I haven't slept in a while. I will sleep; after all, I have stopped using the body lotion."

I don't want to go ahead to tell you that it got to the point that she couldn't sleep any longer. When she finally went to see the doctor, she spent more than she would have in the early days of the occurrence.

It could have been worse; many fatal cases of cancer in Third World Countries are blamed on late diagnosis which is hinged on the procrastination of patients. This is to show you that procrastination actually cost lives. You probably aren't doing that particular important task right now, because you have convinced yourself that you are reading a book on procrastination for the first time but it is important we define procrastination again, so you recognize it at every turn.

Procrastination is the avoidance or the action of delaying or postponing a task that needs to be accomplished.

Indecision

Sometimes procrastination can be as a result of indecision. These indecisions range from inability to determine what is important to us, to why a particular action or task should be done, or how it should be done. There is a difference between a student studying for his SAT exam, who simply cannot make a decision to either read his books or go partying with friends, and a student who is yet to do his assignment because he simply hasn't decided on the way he will do the assignment. One is a problem of priorities, which, by the way, can be relative because the student sitting for his SAT exam might actually think that partying is his number one priority. However, the student with the assignment is a typical problem of indecision.

Procrastination also arises at a pivotal point between deciding what to do because of the uncertainty of the outcome, or when there are a whole lot of alternative ways to get the job done.

Are we going to fail? Or succeed?

The unconscious inability to answer this question dampens our morale in finishing tasks. For example, in an attempt to make the maiden edition of the school annual magazine spectacular, the editor in chief – a student - had decided to interview president Donald Trump. She had drafted a letter, sealed it, and it was ready to be mailed. She had also gotten the phone details of the chief of staff to the president while not forgetting to collect the official email address of the office of the president. But for weeks, she couldn't use any of the mediums that were made available for her because she was not sure of the particular one that would be more efficient.

The Inspiration And Motivation Myth

Humans have a tendency to act on the basis of inspiration. Every single action is backed by inspiration, and this inspiration can either be positive or negative. It's interesting to know that even procrastination has its own inspiration. A particular set of psychologists in the United States, with the use of Neuro-linguistic Programming (NLP), have successfully harnessed the concept of procrastination in anger management, this they do by teaching their clients on how to procrastinate anger and depression. But before they can do this, they tend to get the patient inspired and motivated to want to get rid of anger. Here is a perfect example of riding procrastination on the back of inspiration.

The creative industry tends to be a perfect example of where inspiration is a reason why people procrastinate. It is believed that it is impossible for a poet to write a poem, a singer to pen down songs and for a painter to paint without inspiration. Therefore, most people decide to go out and chill with friends or engage in other activities with the excuse that they are seeking inspiration. The fact is that the absence of inspiration, or the belief that nothing can be done without a certain level of inspiration, causes procrastination.

Even with inspiration, the absence of motivation will get you nowhere. It is one thing to sit down with the height of inspiration of what to write and another thing to actually write when you want to write a book. When things get terrible, or when you run out of inspiration, you will definitely need to stay motivated in order to get the task done. A humanitarian once journeyed deep into a town in Thailand. The leaders in the community had been expecting her for over a year and asked her why it took her so much time to come finally. She smiled and told them that it was because of procrastination.

Did you read that? A whole year filled with procrastination!

What happened was that the humanitarian had planned her journey to this town early with her motivation being the desire to help in family planning. Along the line, however, she started considering the living conditions she was going to be subjected to in this town, and the difficulty in adapting to life in a new environment. While she was at this level of considerations, she lost motivation: that was the reason why she arrived a year later.

Downplay Of Tasks/Trivialization

Trivialization, which is the act of making something to appear insignificant, can be likened to denial. The difference, however, is that in trivializing; we actually recognize that we are in deep into procrastination. When presented with two or more tasks, we simply tend to downplay the more important, or the more demanding ones as totally being unimportant. Take the dermatologist, for example, trivializing a potential visit to his office will mean that I am downplaying the importance of seeing the doctor. But denial, on the other hand, means that I actually recognize that seeing a doctor is important, but I am yet to see him.

Trivialization does not just affect the important tasks; it also affects the not so important tasks. The cat you do not feed before leaving the house because it didn't seem important; the task you couldn't do because there was no reward and even the poem you couldn't write because you felt that nobody would read it after all. If at the edge of getting a task done, we trivialize it, there is a likely probability that our initial conclusion will cloud our sense of judgment. For example, as a student, if you are given an assignment that you regarded as not important because you need to hang out with your friends, there is a probability that you will not get back to that assignment.

Lack Of Rewards

Most times the wheels of the motivation to get the job done are filled with rewards that can be gotten from the job. Rewards cut across different definitions. They could be monetary, gratification, satisfaction or a sense of belonging. If faced with tasks that require equal attention, there is a great tendency that we will complete the one with a greater reward before any other one. Let's say you are an architect and you have a task to design three structures for three different clients, the first task will bring you a lot of recognition, and it will be a boost for your career, but the monetary reward is low. The second one has a lot of monetary rewards, but it won't bring you recognition. And the third one will bring you both recognition and a lot of money. It is a common intuitive that you will go after the one with greater reward while relegating other ones to the background. The case of choosing a task with greater rewards is mostly a result of having overwhelming tasks at hand. If a student is given two different assignments, despite the fact that his reward is not in money, he will perform the tasks because of the rewards of mental satisfaction that would come later. Rewards do not, however, justify procrastination, as it is a relative factor. It is a relative factor such that sometimes, when the rewards are too much, it can actually freak the individual out, leading to procrastination too.

Perfectionism

The fear of having to do something and it turns out not to be perfect to put a whole lot of pressure on people. Perfectionism contributes to procrastination. We either aren't doing a particular task because we are waiting for the perfect time to get a perfect output, or simply because we don't want to do it at that point or any other time; this is rampant among people who are perfectionists. Another example of procrastination that arises as a result of perfectionism is performing a task halfway. Some people will refrain from performing a task if there is no possibility of finishing that task. This is because they like finishing what they start. Pete, a fictional character, will rather not start something if he would not be able to finish it. Thus, when he is faced with such tasks, he freaks out.

Distraction

Mankind has never been so exposed to as many distractions as what we are currently experiencing in the 21st century. Social media, news media, movies, mobile phones, music, etc. and all other sources of distraction you can think of, contribute to procrastination. I am sure we can all relate to this. We have all experienced situation where we had to postpone a particular task just because there was a certain

WhatsApp or Facebook message we had to reply or a particular trend or Twitter that we simply couldn't ignore. We are in a generation where the smartphone is now the closest companion of man, but enough of the new trend of distraction. The truth is that even before the arrival of these technological advancements, there was a distraction. Distractions like emotional distractions; responsibilities to the society; and the family, extra-curricular activities and many others are perfect examples free from the pendulum of the 21st-century technology.

Studies show that students who tend to be easily distracted are the ones that hardly get their assignment done. Also, most students that get easily distracted are either from a broken home or are experiencing emotional problems. Apart from subjective distractions, other tasks that might seemingly be important at that point in time distract us. For example, a friend while working on a proposal for his company sometimes ago experienced some challenges with a leaky faucet that caused him to be distracted. After they called the local technician to fix the fault, he realized that he had a relatively small amount of time to finish the proposal for the company; he had unconsciously postponed the processes of getting the work done. Distractions!

The Fear Of Success

As strange as it might seem, sometimes we tend to procrastinate because we are scared of the responsibilities that come with success. It is common knowledge that with success comes a bigger expectation.

Maybe the only reason why that very talented singer has been postponing his chance to record his first studio song is that he is scared the song will shoot him to spotlight, a life he is not ready to live just yet. There is no contradicting to the fact that you would not belong to the same circle that you once belonged to when you were not successful. Success would mean taking on more responsibilities than you can shoulder. In the case of relationships, it may be that a delay in getting married is caused by the fear of the responsibilities that would come with jumping the broom with your partner.

Rebellion

This is a subtle reason why people procrastinate. It can simply be a tactic to go against some certain rules or standards in an organization, or simply due to external evaluation. Procrastination may be a form of rebelling against people. When a friend was younger, his uncle grounded him for two weeks because he was out late. Three days later, the same uncle gave my friend his shoes to clean for him. On a normal day, my friend would have cleaned the shoes without having a second thought, but being grounded for two weeks meant he was going to miss playing video games with my friends. Because of that, he didn't clean the shoes because he simply wanted to rebel against his uncle. Also, there are cases like a student failing his courses intentionally simply because he didn't like the school he was put in. That student would have postponed the performance of academic tasks like assignment and tests. Employees in companies rebel against management by procrastinating their duties. There have been reports of strikes being held by labor unions of the Hollywood movie industry in order to rebel against the directors that refused to pay what had been agreed upon in their contracts.

Unassertiveness

Being unassertive makes us agree to do things that we don't really want to do. Having to do unreasonable tasks just because we cannot simply say "no" can get us pretty overwhelmed with so much work that our only way out is procrastination? Few years' back, a friend gave his nephew a task to do on the computer with Microsoft Excel, thinking he was familiar with it. The nephew, on the other hand, accepted to do the task, not wanting to say no to his aunt because she had promised to get him a gift once he is done. In the end, she got to know that in the quest to get this particular task done, he spent time learning how to use MS Excel. This affected his school assignments and other house chores to the extent that he started waking up very late because he was mostly doing his research into the night. His inability to say "no" didn't just end up in him procrastinating the task she gave to him, but it also led to the procrastination of other important things that he could have done without stress. Many people tend to fall in this category: "the fear of the unknown" when we simply refuse a task, grips us so much that we accept anything that is thrown our way because we want to win approval.

Reframing

Reframing has to do with leaving a particular task undone until the rush hour; believing that doing the work at an early stage will do harm to the expected output. It is one of the prevalent excuses that aid procrastination. For example, I might have a deadline to get a task done in one day, but due to my past experience and knowing that I tend to work better in the midnight, I will skip working on the task in the afternoon and even in the evening; many people have been in this situation. The strange thing about reframing is that it can form a routine that tends to develop into a habit. For example, being a worker living in a city with so much traffic gridlock, a person may be always getting back to his apartment late. After having his bath, he eats and watches the news update, after which he turns on his computer to work on tasks that need to be worked on. This became a routine, and the person may begin to find it difficult to work immediately after he gets back from work without eating or taking his bath- not even without watching the news update. The most definitive of it all was that such people had conditioned their minds to only work after doing the normal routine. This is harmful because failure to get it done at this unhealthy time will mean they are not going to beat the deadline. Reframing is also common among students who start reading their books days to their exams believing that starting early will lead to them forgetting what they have read during tests and examinations.

Laziness

Laziness comes in different folds. It is generally the quality of the inability to work. The word 'Laziness' over the years have been associated with poverty. Many people are lazy not because they were born lazy, but because they have no sense of direction as to what to do, or simply because they know what they ought to do, but they aren't doing it. Sometimes we procrastinate tasks; just because we do not in any way, have intentions of carrying out these tasks. I believe I can use an example that we can all relate to. Have you ever had to wake up from sleep knowing fully well that you have to get up from the bed in order not to be late for work, but you find yourself still lying on the bed? In some cases, there are times people wake up, and they just cannot believe that it is morning yet. They then convince themselves that they could get some extra bout of sleep for an extra twenty minutes, and go back to sleep. This habit of postponement is not one that is present in the lives of some people and absent in others; rather all successful people encounter this and sometimes fall to the nudge. There are some days that Bill Gates would feel the need to stay back in bed for some hours and allow other people take charge of the daily tasks for the day since he is the richest man on earth. There are days that athletes would feel the need to flunk practice and spend quality time in bed or engaging in other activities.

Lack Of Energy

We need the energy to do work. To finish tasks, we have to be active and productive, and there is nothing that affects the productivity of humans more than anything that affects their energy level. Ill health, poor eating diet, lack of sleep and many others are a major determinant of our energy levels. We tend to function less efficient in moments of our low energy, and the best option that appeals to us becomes procrastination.

In numerous occasions, growing cases of obesity may contribute towards bringing you to the point where you procrastinate on a very frequent basis. Karma , they say, is like a mobile Insurance guy who keeps coming back to visit your door and in this instance, the consumption of too much coke on a daily basis in addition to eating numerous junk foods like pizza, burgers, etc. will eventually contribute towards helping you to procrastinate on a more frequent basis than ever. Perhaps, if you had tried to live a little bit healthier by sticking to veggies and a healthy routine, the procrastination would have been avoided. Sometimes it is actually hard to diagnose these ailments, so it is advised that just maybe, the reason why you procrastinate is hinged on a medical condition that can only be diagnosed by a specialist.

Negativity

Negativity on its own clutters the mind. There is no way we can get a particular task done when we expect the worst output. Sometimes, it is not even the output that causes procrastination but the path taken to get the task done. For example, if as a construction engineer, you are to travel a long distance to get building equipment with a negative mindset, you might end up filing your mind with things like the possibility of an accident, the possibility of getting robbed on your way, the possibility of not getting exactly what you want and even the possibility of you failing as a construction engineer in that particular project. And so in order to avert this negativity, you procrastinate.

Lack Of Patience

Some tasks like writing a movie script, directing a movie or even farming can take so much time in preparation and also, an even longer time for fruition. Some come with so much hardship and difficulty that without patience, we tend to procrastinate or simply not do the job. In those cases, some distinguished screenwriters had to admit this is one of the famous reason as to why they procrastinated in getting a script ready for production. Javed Akhtar, who happens to be a legendary screenwriter in his Tedx talk stated that lack of patience was a potent reason why he had streams of abandoned projects while he continued to move on to newer projects. On some particular occasions, lack of patience can make him abandon a task even after starting since the particular fuelling drive that caused him to begin, seemed to fizzle out. This is very easy to understand unlike Rocket science: just like that time you began an early morning jog and began to enjoy it at the beginning stage. The thrill of feeling the gentle wind hit your face accompanied by the music playing from your headphone may fuel you to keep jogging for more than thirty minutes but when you begin to reach an hour, the real stress sets in. After the thrill comes to the stressful feelings for this task and it is at that point that most runners begin to feel the overwhelming desire to stop to catch their breaths especially if they are engaging in a marathon. This thrill can be found within many homes during the weekends when the father may set out to do the laundry and clean up in the home. In such instances, the father may wake up with so much enthusiasm to get the job done so that in the end, the house would be sparkling clean. But the twist is that just midway into the cleanup, that dad would realize that he had spent more than two hours cleaning and things begin to spiral out of the range of his control. It is at that point that he may begin to feel the need to go out to the park with his dog or go to the pub to catch up with his old friend who tends the bar there. The interesting thing is that he may even begin to think about dumping the job halfway, getting into his car with his family and then zoom off to the cinema to see the latest Avengers film. That is the nature of how the mind works concerning some tasks. I do not believe the mind of anyone can be sufficiently stimulated to begin a task and then finish the task using the same driving force that propelled the start even if the task was a favorite hobby. You may have heard some seasoned bikers go into the tattoo shop with the aim of getting a scary looking tattoo, and then begin to feel the need to leave during the process of getting the tattoo. This particular thing can even be found within couples that choose to engage in a task together. At a point in time, the zeal of continue will come due to lack of patience, and they may feel the need to engage in procrastination.

It Might Be Beyond Procrastination

Do you feel tired when it comes to the period that you wish to engage in a task that may be grueling? Perhaps that task may be skipping due to your need to lose weight or maintain that hourglass figure of yours. Away from procrastination, it is possible that what seems to be procrastination might be a symptom to something serious. Procrastination has previously been linked with hypertension, cardiovascular disease, bipolar disorder, and anxiety issues. Also, procrastination may be the offshoot of that terrible mental ailment called Depression. We all know what it means to be depressed. That period of time when nothing seems to appeal to you and every task becomes a bore. In some cases, such depression may be so crippling because they arise from a feeling of un-fulfillment. Just like in the case of every successful person, they would be faced with those times when they would be filled with feelings of not reaching their potentials: some medical personnel would call this 'Mid-life crisis.' Nevertheless, if you begin to notice that you procrastinate often, a visit to the counselor or psychologist may be good so that you are able to identify the issue and nip it in the bud immediately.

Now, I am not saying to jump up and rush off to a psychologist at just the slightest tinge of feeling down and out. This is more serious than that. A seasoned helping hand who is trained should come in to intervene when you are feeling almost energy-less. The day feels sooo long yet you are loathe to actually do anything. Even thoughts of doing anything feel you with such overpowering weariness that you just want to continue lying down in that couch or stay in bed. When thoughts of mortality creep in, then it is most definitely time to seek professional, medically trained help.

CHAPTER 3 :
THE MEAT OF THINGS 36 WAYS PROVEN

36 Proven Ways To Help Anyone Beat Procrastination

Goal Setting And Monitoring

The goal of writing this book on procrastination is to take you to a point where even the thought of procrastination begins to seem repulsive to your thoughts, and that is why it is important to set goals and monitor the progress of such goals. Goals are particular tasks that you have deliberately written down and placed in a strategic point that is easily accessible for you to see. Examples of such goals may be;

I want to be the greatest showman in the circus I am working now

I want to be the greatest vet doctor and the best friend to all pets

I want to become the next President of the United States of America.

I want to be the best Talk-show host that the world has ever seen.

All these are great goals that many people have set over the course of the years, and they have been reached after much perseverance. The key to happy living and avoiding procrastination is setting a goal that is realistic. By realistic, I mean that you should set a goal that has a definite time frame and can be broken down into smaller parts. For example, if you set the goal of becoming the best in your ballet class, the goal can be broken down to little tasks that would help you reach it steadily. Those little tasks must be spelled out in explicit details and placed in strategic places around your home. For example, you can write,

"Ballet lessons by 5."

"Jogging time by 7."

You can easily get a sticker and paste these two on your fridge so you can easily see them and be reminded of their importance. However, you would have to ensure that you follow through with them by being strict with your time consumption.

Goal Monitoring is a task that has been engaged in by the greatest achievers in the world. An achiever like Oprah Winfrey was so dedicated to monitoring the goals that she always engaged in getting feedback from her close circle on her progress in her career as a Talk-show host. While this may seem to be awkward to other people who see her as already successful, the only way to become more successful, for her, is to engage in a constant critique of her performance that would show her progress. This process also enabled her to defeat the negative habit of procrastination.

It is pointless trying to avoid procrastination when you do not have a goal that you are chasing. Generally speaking, everyone either ends up achieving their personal goals or the goals of other people. While this may sound shallow, it remains the truth because you can either employ your efforts to helping yourself become the best or help other people become the best by choosing to remain rooted in your spot. Find your goal today and make sure that they are well spelled out so that you are easily motivated towards chasing them.

Do not Feel Comfortable with Your Level of Success

How much do you think you have achieved? The answer to this would greatly determine how much you procrastinate because people who generally feel comfortable with their status do not feel the need to advance and then begin to procrastinate more.

Let us take the example of an athlete like Mike Tyson. The Boxing profession is one that requires the fighters to give it every shot and attention on their way to the top. Being a boxer who yearned to reach the top, Mike Tyson could never afford to procrastinate about the time for engaging in early morning and evening jogs. Since he needed to build his punching skills, he could not afford to procrastinate about hitting the gym because he needed to engage in intense workout sessions with the punching bag. Also, need to learn the best way to anticipate any opponent he would face in the ring, Tyson never procrastinated when the time to fight other gym fighters and his trainer, arose. Through his lack of procrastination and strict adherence to his regimen, Tyson was able to keep rising through the ranks at even the expense of other fighters who were more talented than him. At a certain stage in his career when he had reached the top and was sufficiently well known after fighting Evander Holyfield, Tyson began to lose focus and then procrastination sets in.

You should never feel comfortable with your level of success because when you do, you will immediately lose focus and an up starter, who keeps taking everything into detail without procrastination, will upstage you. Imagine that you were a pop-singer and you have risen through the ranks from playing at local theme parks to have sold out concerts and winning the Grammy awards. At that point when you have won the Grammys, it would seem that you have reached the pinnacle of your career. Most pop stars would then begin to procrastinate on the time for rehearsals or procrastinate when they need to attend important meetings with their sponsors. This procrastination begins to build up and cause the pop star to fall off the favor list of the fan base, and if there is no source of stimulant, such a pop star may fall back into obscurity. That is the reason why you should always continue to discover better ways to stimulate yourself

One of the excellent ways to avoid feeling too comfortable is when you begin to place value on getting rid of pain and humanitarian challenges in the world. Take the example of Bill Gates who has always been on the list of the richest men in the world. In his case, he has set up companies that would continue to bring income for him and can afford to procrastinate, but he sought out a new challenge that he devotes his time to face now. The challenge he chose and is pumping many funds into is the alleviation of poverty from numerous Third World Countries through the provision of health facilities, portable water, the sound educational structure as well as sustainable energy creation. Through the Bill and Melinda foundation, you can easily see how he uses the new challenge to defeat procrastination.

Understand That Your Talent Will Not Guarantee Your Success

The graveyard is often referred to as the greatest treasure place on earth. The sentiment is echoed across different cultures in the world, and the reason is very clear; it is the resting place of people who never achieved their full potential. People who think that they are talented and that is enough end up becoming the worst procrastinators who do not reach anywhere. Every child is very talented in one aspect of life while some can exhibit numerous talents in many fields.

However, what happens when you think that talent is enough? The answer is that the person begins a downward spiral into procrastination. If you get to watch sports on a regular basis, you may hear the sportscaster make mention of lines like, "here is the new Wayne Gretzky" for those who are hockey enthusiasts. If you were watching the tennis game, you might have heard the sportscaster state that a certain player was the "New Roger Federer" or the "Heir to the throne of Borg and McEnroe." The reason why such sportscasters may have said it is that such players exhibit great gifts that would be able to propel them towards becoming personal greats in the game. However, the bitter truth is that a significant amount of such players often fall off the radar because they believed in their gifts too much and began to make procrastination when it was time for training.

Which talents do you have that has attracted the attention of people? You should be careful with the praise and understand that your gift is not the only ingredient that would make you succeed. You must be able to develop a strict routine of activities that will help you build your talents. Presidents such as George Bush, Barack Obama were not born; rather, they recognized some leadership talents at a little age and began to consciously set down routines that were meant to help them rise through the political ranks until they were eventually elected into the White House.

Let Technology Help

We are in the global age wherein ideas continue to transform into workable projects and ultimately become the new technology that drives our society. There are now technological applications for almost everything, and there are apps that can help you beat your habit of procrastination. Have you ever heard of BZ Reminder? It is an application that can easily be downloaded via Google Playstore and you can begin to use it to overcome procrastination. So how does it work exactly? To begin, you would need to mentally organize yourself through the identification of your goals as well as breaking them down into actionable routine actions.

After you have done that, you then begin by inputting every action that you intend to take at the particular time that you want to take it. There is an option where you get to write down notes, and this will be vital in case you will need that note to remind you of the dire need of the action. After doing this, you then save the actions and the application would begin to issue out prompt reminders to you at every point in time. Other applications that engage in this are Wunderlist, Life Reminders, Remember the Milk and others. Reminders are very vital as they serve as the stimulant that tells you what needs to be done and reminds you to get your butt up.

Other technological advancements that can monitor the level at which you are reaching your goals, help to serve as tools that enable you to ward off procrastination. For example, Samsung Health, which is a pre-installed application on Samsung devices, help the owners to be able to monitor the number of steps that they have taken in a particular day. In most cases, individuals who wish to engage in a weight reduction routine and adopt jogging or power walks, make use of Samsung Health that they can use to create a target for themselves. A beautiful aspect of the application is its alarm feature that informs the user that the daily target has been reached or not. With a reminder like that, it becomes very difficult to procrastinate.

Get To The Root Why Are Procrastinating

Do you know what usually happens when you go to a dentist with a tooth that you desperately want to remove because the pain it is giving you? The dentist would begin the procedure by checking other teeth that are close by before focusing on the tooth that is making you feel dis-comfortable. The same thing applies to other Medical Doctors who tend to ask you questions that may seem to be totally irrelevant to you but hold the most answers for the doctor.

The reason they do this is that they wish to determine the root cause of the sickness because it may spring up another sickness if the present is cured. Just like the way obesity is the root cause of numerous heart related medical challenges, there is a particular root cause that is causing you to engage in so much procrastination.

One of the most devastating root causes is a type of Temperament you have. There are basically four major temperaments that every human being falls into, and they are;

1. Sanguine

2. Phlegmatic

3. Choleric

4. Melancholic.

Every reader of this book must make a conscious effort to discover what their temperament is and then research on the ways they can manage them. The major temperament many chronic procrastinators fall into is Sanguine. The Sanguine is a person that can be the life of the party and may be someone who loves to aspire. However, the major challenge with the Sanguine is that she or he gets easily disinterested in activities and relationships. While a Sanguine guy may initiate a relationship with a lady and seem to be smitten by her, he may begin to show disinterest as the days go by and the same happens vice versa. If a Sanguine was to aspire to become the greatest drama writer after William Shakespeare, she would begin the process of writing with much enthusiasm and would experience true happiness at the beginning stages, however, as the days roll by, and the thrill disappears, while another temperament like Melancholic will retain a staunch focus to complete the work, the Sanguine would shelve the work and move on to the next interesting thing while procrastinating that she would return to work at a later date. Unfortunately, the Sanguine is often filled with too many projects that are screaming for completion, but she is still chasing newer ones. If you recognize that you are a Sanguine, you should begin to engage in extensive research that would enable you to manage your temperament as well as overcome the challenge of procrastination.

Another root cause of Procrastination is fear. Fear is one of the most dangerous killers in the world because it delights in early truncation of projects that have reached halfway. There are many individuals who wished to become wildlife photographers that would be popular enough to work at the National Geographic, but they never ventured further because of fear. In such instances, they may become afraid of the hazards that may come with exploring the Amazon or getting close enough to take pictures of Polar Bears. In some other instances, other people have abandoned their dreams of becoming top Class chefs because they are afraid of the nature of reception that they would receive from people who would taste their meals.

In both cases, fear has made those individuals engage in a series of prolonged procrastination until they eventually drop such goals in pursuit of other. Everyone harbors fear at one point or the other, but the achievers always face their fear head-on since they recognize the need not to procrastinate. Successful business tycoons such as Tony Robbins who has made millions out of the practice of Networking tell that when faced with fears, he does not flinch at all. Rather, he walks up to the individual he intends to pitch to and begins without fear. The reason is that there is absolutely nothing to lose when you try and fail. However, when you do not try at all, you have everything to lose since there is a possibility that you could have overcome. Another excellent way which one can overcome such fear is when you build up a practice of repeating self-affirmative words over time. This has proved to be a very potent confidence booster while it enhances people's belief in their capacity to take on every task. Identify the root cause of your procrastination today and begin to deal with them.

Get A Coach

There is absolutely nowhere you can get to in life without the help of others, and there are very limited heights you can reach without a mentor or a coach to guide you. When taking on the task of defeating the enemy called Procrastination, you will surely need all the help you can get.

Who are your mentors? Members of some interviewing boards sometimes ask that question because the answer to such a question can help them form a quick opinion about you and your motivations. To identify your mentor/coach, you must take your time and never choose based on personal sentiments arising from your relationship with the person.

In most cases, many people choose their parents as mentors and end up procrastinating because their coach has not been able to overcome procrastination. Choose a person who is insanely dedicated to their work and has been successful in the career. This means that if you are pursuing the goal of becoming a musical artist in the genre of New Age Music, you can get Enya and Yanni to be your mentors as they would be able to provide you with information on how to conquer procrastination as your career advances. However, on some occasions like the one previously stated, you may choose a mentor that is not easily accessible and that is why you should work toward getting a coach that can be easily accessible.

Boxers wisely choose their coach because their coaches are the ones that come, looking to drag them away from their homes when the fighter begins to procrastinate. In your case, you should always inquire from your coach on the best way to be stimulated enough to overcome procrastination because that is the best way to overcome. While many Top 500 Forbes companies adopt the measure of deadlines to stimulate their employees into completing projects, that kind of stimulation may not work for individual human beings. Ask your coach to teach you the best way to set deadlines for yourself that you will be able to work towards with the same vigor you would adopt if you were at your workplace.

Join Arduous Tasks With Pleasant Ones

One of the easiest ways to get discouraged and begin to adopt the act of procrastination is when you separate easier tasks from the difficult ones. In the course of achieving any goal that you set, there would be the easier ones that would give you an immediate thrill when you finish engaging in them, along with the difficult ones that can be physically and mentally draining. Your goal will be to do the hard tasks immediately after the easier ones so that the thrill can stimulate you enough to tackle it.

Let's assume that you are harboring the intent of writing an important professional exam that will bring you a promotion at your job and you need to take both Statistics and an English exam. Let's imagine that you someone who is totally inclined to the arts but find the statistics course to be mentally challenging and nothing you do seems to be working. Naturally, what happens is that you may begin to passively postpone the period of reading your Statistics books because they frankly bring you no joy while you relish the time spent with your English books. You can overcome your procrastination and get it right by choosing to read your Statistics immediately after you drop your English book. The reason is that it has been scientifically proven that your brain is more excited when you try out enjoyable things and this can enable it to pick the more difficult things immediately while it is still flooded with the feel-good dopamine.

You will have to make the self-conscious decision of writing down the most enjoyable tasks which you have to engage in and the 'most annoying jobs I would rather not face but must be done.' Penning them down in a detailed manner is the first step.

The next would be to pair them together in order to ensure that complimentary tasks go together. If you are into web designing and have to learn how to code using JavaScript and the likes, you will have to fix the time for coding, which a few web developers do not like to do, along with the time for designing on paper. This is because it is thrilling to design how the website would look on paper and the dopamine that is released during that moment can be used to attack difficult tasks such as coding. I have discovered as well that the most people who make the killing gains on the Forex market are those that forecast immediately after making a huge profit. At that point, they are able to shed off some form of restraints of fear and buy the shares while adopting some form of caution as well.

Do Not Try To Overstretch Yourself On Tasks

The simple truth that is being said here is, don't overtask yourself.

Frankly, you are not an automated machine that can perform a billion tasks at a given time. Even automated machines can run into bigger problems when they are taxed to engage in the tasks that they have not been programmed to do, so slow down.

You cannot become everything. That fact is very vital for you to understand today because so many people are stressing themselves over becoming many things and then get to realize that they are failing badly at most of them because they are procrastinating.

Imagine you meet a lady who is training to become a Black Belt holder in Taekwondo, studying to become a ballet dancer, studying to become a financial expert and also trying to become a screenwriter. I know that you may be so much surprised and feel that she is awesome but in reality, she will be struggling with avoiding procrastination since most of the tasks would require her to focus on them.

If she chooses to focus on screenwriting as well as Taekwondo strictly, she would be able to effortlessly manage herself and draw up concrete plans that she can focus on achieving without overstretching herself. Your ultimate goal should not be to acquire as numerous titles as you can in reaching the top but to acquire one and work your butt off to becoming excellent in that field.

Take the case of Steve Jobs, the co-founder of Apple: he could have chosen to take on his tasks by singing with a band, but he did not. Instead, he focused daily on building tasks that were solely within his niche and worked tirelessly at achieving those goals he set. Today, Apple has broken through the One Trillion dollar valuation margin, and it is mainly thanks to one man who chose to stick to one task.

Let us take a scenario that you may be more familiar with. Have you ever seen an Olympic 100 meters race? The thing you notice is that each athlete has a special lane set up for him or her. The white line that separates them mainly defines these tracks, and you notice that when the gun pops, each athlete begins to run within their lane so as to avoid reaching the finish line in another person's lane that attracts disqualification. Usain Bolt won all his titles by sticking to his lane and not crossing into the lane of other contenders like Asafa Powell, Tyson Gay, Justin Gatlin, and the likes. The immediate lesson that you can get is that there are no gains for running in too many directions. Often, such people do not end up reaching the finish line of any of the directions because they would have procrastinated so much.

Don't Beat Yourself Over What You Cannot Change

There are some things that won't change so don't get frustrated by trying to change them. You will have to recognize this fast in order not to engage in tasks that would be extremely frustrating for you and make you engage in the act of procrastination.

The general idea is that you should find a goal that you have a passion for and then begin to engage in it with much vigor. However, during the course of reaching your destination, you will meet with some challenges that you cannot solve and will have to adopt the option of letting them go.

For example, in the course of building your team that will spur you to achieve your goals, you will recognize some team members who are going to slow the group down considerably because of their inefficiency. There are other team members that may be very brilliant but have terrible character traits that they are unwilling to change. In such cases, you will have to let the two sets of employees go so that you can be able to advance speedily towards achieving the group goals. This has to be done so you don't expend much energy trying to change what such group members may be unwilling to change.

Seasoned achievers like Steve Jobs easily recognized this fact and began to apply them at an early stage of their business. They first began to scrutinize the ideology of their would-be employee or team members. When they ascertain that a group member is not on par or is not motivated, they immediately pull the plug on the involvement of such team members in order to keep the team morale high. They did this particular action when it involved their family members because they realized that there was no place for personal sentiments in building a unique brand.

Also, if you are in the practice of trying to salvage a relationship that is going off the rocks and the other party keeps dragging it down with a force of habit, it is time you consider pulling the plug. For example, if you are in a relationship that is perpetually filled with accounts of domestic violence that seems not to have an end, you should try and work it out with the partner and then leave if the partner is not showing promising signs of changing.

The reason you have to leave is that your sanity and esteem are very important and you do not need to continue remaining frustrated as time goes by. Within frustration lies the seed of procrastination as it becomes easy for you to lose focus of the most important part of your goals while you try to change something that will never change.

Filter Your Options And Choose One

For every challenge that comes your way, there are a plethora of options that present themselves as potential answers. However, in order to avoid giving room to procrastination, stick to one option and work hard at it until you become excellent at it.

Let us examine Nations as an example, with the Nation of Israel being the case study.

The Zionist movement that comprises of the Jewish people identified a problem that was the fact that the Jews had no homeland, and then began to work towards buying up lands in Palestine progressively. Ever since the Dreyffus affair, most Jews within the areas they lived in Europe experienced intense anti-Semitism riots and disenfranchisement, and all this piled up to the German genocide that was initiated by Adolf Hitler.

Because of the constant persecutions, the richest Jews formed the movement and then proceeded to buy up Palestinian lands where they began to emigrate until they finally gained their independence in 1948. Since that time of their independence, Israel has been actively engaged in one main course of guaranteeing her continued survival that is through the building of their defense ministry through military buildup. Till date, they continue to pump a large number of funds into the acquisition of the latest military technology while also building her missile detection systems so as to avoid any form of external attacks.

Any observer can easily see that Israel could have chosen to stick to diplomacy to achieve her aims, but she chose to adopt the option of the military buildup in order to deter any form of action against them. On the other hand, the Palestinians have a noble cause but have been deterred because they are chasing too many options. While the Palestinian Liberation Organization chases the more peaceful and diplomatic way of getting a Palestinian state through the United Nations, the Hamas has continued to engage in a series of terror attacks against the Israeli and these terror attacks serve to undermine the efforts which the PLO has been engaging in.

The idea that is espoused here is that you should stick to one option and hone it into perfection. Sometimes, this process would take years, but the most successful people have taken years to master their craft. Take a look at Tiger Woods who identified the particular sport he was good in and began to focus on reaching the top. Becoming an excellent golfer is a mastery that takes years to perfect, and that is the exact thing that Tiger Woods did. You do not have the luxury of time to keep exploring option ever because you may discover that none works since you did not give it enough time to explore. Develop a key principle of Patience.

Get Rid Of Distractions Both Digital And Human

There is absolutely no way you can reach the top by taking note of every little thing that happens around you. Athletes like Mo Faran who are engaged in marathon races are always so focused on running that they are not even deterred by natural phenomenon. When racing through the designated route, they do not stop to take selfies with excited fans or stop to engage in other things because distraction brings loss of focus and then ultimately leads to failures. This brings us to the first point that you will have to clear out every mental distraction.

A Formula, One racer like Sebastian Vettel, cannot afford to come into the race with the mindset that he will lose the game and the same thing happens for individuals across all sports except the ones that are scripted like Wrestling.

Other mental cobwebs that you will have to clear out within your mind are factors like low self-esteem which is harboring the thought that you are not good enough to engage in a task: What often happens is that such an individual begins to falter and then falls into a vicious cycle of procrastination that may bring failure at the end.

After you have sufficiently cleared your mental obstacles, the next sets are the physical obstacles starting with technology.

While technology has been a source of blessing to mankind as we have been able to achieve phenomenal feats in the fields of Artificial intelligence, Nanotechnology as well as other technologies that are boosting human relations, it has served to be one of the greatest drawbacks as there are more than enough applications which can derail individuals from achieving their goals.

Let us take, for example, the case of little kids and video games. That is an aspect where parents are still finding very difficult to communicate their desires to the kids. For example, a kid that is playing God of War and is so engrossed in it would not be happy when reminded of the need to eat food. The parents of that kid would even find it greatly difficult to get that kid to perform his school homework, as the kid would keep postponing it. One of the ways that the parent can help that kid is to take away those video games for a while and even though the child would sulk for longer periods of time, the parent would be able to get him to do his homework.

If you are a college student, you would understand the reason why technology provides the greatest source of an obstacle. Social media applications like Facebook, Instagram, YouTube, and Vine preoccupy the attention of many college students who are constantly seeking to connect better with friends or become more popular. Viral challenges have also been the cause of procrastination as social media users are so obsessed with joining in the train without paying attention to their personal career paths. If your career path aligns with the use of social media, you would need to engage in these, but if you are not chasing a career along that part, you will have to drastically cut short your use of the social media in order to focus on reaching your goals. Seasoned winners have understood this fact and ensure that they hire social media managers in order to avoid getting caught up with social media because it will bring about procrastination into the time that should be used for other profitable pursuits.

Another distraction that you need to put away is human distractions. Human beings have generally been wired to seek after companionship at some point in their lives, and even though there is the need to build up a network of friends that would be around you to support you at most times that you are down or celebrate with you, you would need to learn how to be lonely at times. This is because friendships can become the cause for your procrastination.

Let us say that you are a web developer who has been given a fresh project to work on by a very reputable tech company at Silicon Valley. When such companies give out jobs like that, they expect that the individual finishes it on time. Now, let us assume that you have a group of friends who call you up and complain that you have not been frequent at the spa and wished to come to your home to pick you up. The immediate thought that may come to you is "Why not?" and then you may mentally begin to shelve away the plans that you have during the night while relishing an opportunity to be among friends. However, a truly successful person would have to politely say no to the invitation and stand firmly by her decision because she recognizes the fact that she needs to engage in a grueling session of coding so as to finish up with the project given to her.

Let us say you have just become a parent, and you are at home with your newborn. At that time, you may feel the urge to go out for a period of time and come back to attend to your baby's laundry. If you give in to such thought, you would only be piling up the jobs that you need to do, and you may not get to perform such jobs perfectly. The most successful people have cultivated the habit of being lonely because they realize that they get most inspiration at such moments and are able to cheer themselves the more. If you are a sports player who enjoys the cheering and the company of people who adore you, you may need to begin detaching yourself from them at some point because they may keep reminding you of your unique abilities while you forget to perform the activities that got earned you the top spot in the first place.

Get Rid of Indecision

There has been no other pathetic sight that I have seen than a person who is seen to take much time contemplating if to take one action or not. In the classic film, A man on a Ledge, the protagonist finds his way through to the top of a high building and then stands on the ledge with the threat to jump to his death more than 60 feet above the ground level. Like all suicide attempts, a crowd began to gather, and most of them urged him not to take his life. Rather, they appealed that he should look on life with fresh vigor and come down. As the hours passed by, the pleas that he should not commit suicide, eventually turned into angry chants that he should jump to his death since he was taking a long time in deciding to jump. At the ending part of the film plot, however, viewers saw that he had no intent to die as he served as a distraction while his gang engaged in the theft of a diamond from a new-by office. However, the immediate lesson learned is that people get impatient over the course of time when you exhibit indecision.

In the same vein, indecision can cost you a lot of opportunities because people will get frustrated and end up passing you. To a pressing extent, indecision is the cause that causes procrastination, and you can easily see it among college students who are in their finals.

Many of such students begin to experience panic when they are told to state their future career path and when they exhibit indecision, they begin to procrastinate in engaging in the right set of activities that they need to take.

For example, a college student who has not yet decided between choosing to pursue a legal career or follow through with her passion of photography will continue to postpone the decision of getting a professional camera and applying for summer internships at reputable photography agencies. The line of thinking that often spurs such indecision is that there is enough time. However, you should learn to attach maximum importance to every second of the day so as to avoid indecision.

Imagine that you were thrust into the setting of a horror film where you are presented with the opportunity to either use a chainsaw to fight off zombies or run away. I am very sure that you would carry the chainsaw without waiting for any second. That is the sense of urgency that you must try to adopt at all times. This doesn't mean you should not think through any action before you take it. However, thinking about the action you wish to take must not take long as there are many lives hanging in the balance. To ward off indecision, you should adopt the motto which states that "the earlier, the better." This will enable you to start off with the right decisions at an early stage.

Make Use of Productivity Hacks

In order to be able to defeat procrastination, you can begin to engage the use of some productivity hacks that have been tested and trusted. Two of such hacks are discussed below and are still being adopted by highly successful people.

Time Chunking: According to the seasoned guru, Tony Robbins, chunking is the grouping together of information into ideally sized pieces, so they can be used effectively to produce the outcome you need without stress or shutdown. The idea behind chunking your time is that you are dedicating particular periods of your time in solving the much-needed tasks that need to be done. In most occasions, people tend to run their life tasks in a haphazard format with no thinking considered for chunking. With Time chunking comes orderliness and with orderliness comes precision.

Let us see how you can be able to chunk your time in a wise format.

The first step is that you must be able to capture all your tasks on paper. Your tasks may include, spiritual exercises, health exercises, career building, relationship building, and the list is endless.

When you identify these tasks, you can then proceed to the next stage that is carving out time for all of them in a way that balance will be ensured. To carve out time, you can choose tasks that are complementary in nature and then lump them together

Let me quickly give a quick example of how you can chunk your time.

You can designate certain days of the week to be set aside for jogging so that you do not feel the need to always engage in an early morning jog. Such days can be devoted towards going to the gym and also family building time if you are in a relationship.

On such days, you can totally ignore anything about advancing your career in order to focus on the activity. This makes it less difficult to procrastinate when the days for other tasks arrive because you would be mentally ready to engage in such a task.

For dads and moms who have been postponing the time of bonding with their children, they can set aside particular days and time where they will totally ignore other things and focus on playing with the kids or solve challenges with them. The same applies to pet owners who are noticing that their pets are becoming restless. You can craft out a time that would be beneficial instead of clogging up your time.

However, when you are chunking your time, you must learn to be flexible to make room for activities which may come up at unexpected times.

The Pomodoro Technique is a unique time management technique that is used to break tasks into intervals which is traditionally 25 minutes in order to allow for short breaks. People who tend to go on a long stretch of activities usually end up exhausted at the end when they do not create any kind of interval when they can rest. If you have ever hiked, or engaged in skipping, you would understand what I mean because the two activities can easily start up as enjoyable.

However, when you do not take short breaks to regain your strength, you may find out that the task is terribly boring to you and when the thought of doing them crosses your mind on another day, you will not consider them. Within every task that you are engaging in, learn to break away for some minutes so that your brain can refresh itself with a purpose of attacking the task anew when it returns

Adopt A Mentality That Conquers Fear Of Success

The first step of success usually begins at the doorstep of your mentality. At that door, you will find an entity called fear and your task will be to replace it with boldness. This is because everything you are going to be successful in requires you to picture it.

Every great Athlete who has ever won the Olympic gold medal began to dream of having it and then dealt with the problem of fear.

How then do you deal with the problem of fear and build the right mentality?

To answer that, you have to learn to build up a mental toughness that will later transform into your character. A great pianist like Beethoven had already begun playing at an early age, but he had to develop a mental toughness because of the fear that he may not become the best composer in the world. That is why he was always engaging himself in visualization. Ultimately, what you visualize becomes your reality. If you harbor the thoughts of becoming the best cook in the country that is sought after by 5-star hotels in Las Vegas and Paris, you will have to keep up that image in your head while mentally telling fear to keep quiet.

That fear will whisper everything that could ever go wrong on the path to becoming the greatest chef.

It would remind you of your poor background

It would remind you those moments you cooked and was not appreciated by friends.

It would remind you of the lean pocket and your inability to get enough funds to apply for a cooking show.

That fear may even go as far back as ten years to remind you of an incident when a friend said you would never reach the top.

Fear can be really terrible, and that is why you will have to adopt a mentality that tells fear to shut it. That is the kind of mentality that sees a successful path even within the thick Amazon forest. That is the kind of mentality that sees the impossible and laughs it off. This is the kind of mindset adopted by top researchers at NASA. And top Fortune 500 companies pay a lot of money to hire people with such mentalities.

So What If I Fail?

You should be ready to ask the "*What if I fail question?*

Failure has never meant total closure, and most times, Networkers have often interpreted NO to mean Next Opportunity. Throughout history's course, there have been numerous people who failed and have still gone on to achieve great things in the course of their lives. A classic example of a person that embodies this was Abraham Lincoln who ran for the position of the Presidency on more than one occasion and lost. He was not deterred when he lost but took it as a means to regroup and strategize.

At a point in time when other people were not bothered about the future, Thomas Edison was within his laboratory where he was experimenting with a new invention that was the light bulb. Being a visionary along with Nikolai Tesla, his contemporary, Thomas Edison worked at the light bulb invention for more than a hundred times and kept failing. He could have easily decided to walk away without achieving what he set out to do, but he remained and continued testing. He was finally able to come out with a working design as his name is in the history books now.

Take a drive across your neighborhood, and you are sure to come across a restaurant with the logo of an old man who met with failure in numerous ways. That man was Colonel Sanders, and the restaurant is the Kentucky Fried Chicken that is the fourth largest fast food restaurant chain with over twenty thousand branches across the work.

Colonel Sanders started out late and still encountered numerous rejections for his recipe. Still, he was the kind of person who took NO to mean the next opportunity, and he brushed himself up and went in search of more opportunities.

You may have watched Films like Going in Style, Mandela, and Now You See Me and seen that one of the main actors within the film is an old man nearing his sixties. That man is Morgan Freeman, and he was someone who came to encounter failures till he was reaching his forties. At that period, it was always going to be difficult for him to break into Hollywood but Morgan Freeman's persistence paid off.

If I could go on listing examples of stars who encountered failure. Stars like British Born Andy Murray who had to wait a long time before rising to top the men's tennis world. Stars like JK Rowling who had to endure several rejections until she was able to publish Harry Potter that has become one of the bestselling franchise ever produced. The most important thing you should take note when looking through these examples is that failure is an inevitable part of our lives. Oprah Winfrey did not start off as graceful as she is now but she was ready to fail.

You cannot keep holding on to so much fear of failure that you run away from every attempt. If you are afraid of failing in your relationship, take a risk and begin. You would surely have issues with the guy that you enter the relationship into, but those challenges are the bonds that will unite you both in a more intimate fashion. Most times, failure serves to show you what you did not do right and what you can avoid doing in the next time you try. The right attitude is needed if you are ever going to learn from failing.

Have A Mind Map

Your mind is a unique tool that you will have to train and condition in a certain way so that it can help you in the fight against procrastination instead of working against you. The most successful people have also been the ones who have mastered the art of controlling their minds because they realize the kind of potent weapon it can be for them.

How much have you researched on the human mind? This is vital for you since you need to understand its limits and the best way it can function for you. One of its functions is mind- mapping, and this means the ability of your mind to organize its tasks and then track them mentally. Most people's minds are in a state of chaos with the physical result being the disorganized state that they are and the nature of their procrastination. Being a reader of this book, you should begin to train your mind by engaging in exercises of calm. When you are able to calm your mind, you can beg the process of mapping out the tasks that you wish to do and breaking them down. This brings order to the chaos up in your mind, and the path is paved for concrete directions.

Begin The First 10 Minutes Of What You Have Been Procrastinating On

Since you have been able to identify that fear is inevitable, the next step that to take is to delve into what you have been procrastinating for a period of ten minutes.

Every workshop organized for fiction writers or writers from any other genre always has a session where the lead speaker tell the participants to organize themselves into groups with the intent of putting what they may have learned into practice. After they are spilled, they are given sets of different themes such as "Love," "Betrayal, "Death, etc., to work with, and they are told to be writing everything that comes to their mind for a period of ten minutes without interrupting for any purpose.

This particular way has been known as the freestyle method wherein the writers get to engage in a kind of furious writing of everything that comes to their mind. It is at this point that they allow their subconscious minds take over and this subconscious mind helps to break through the feeling of fear.

This same thing is applicable to budding public speakers who have stage fright and are afraid to speak to large audiences. In order to help them break through this particular fright, an audience may be simulated in a way through technological applications or a live audience may be gotten and the speaker would have to speak for ten minutes. Generally, the ten-minute barrier is set because at that time, you would have begun to gain some form of composure and you would wonder why you had not engaged in the activity beforehand.

Are you part of that group of men who find it difficult to talk to a lady? You do not need the help of intoxicants to dull your senses and embolden you to initiate a conversation. Simply walk up to the lady, say your greetings, and manage a conversation for a period of ten minutes. What you notice is that your mind would stop ticking down to the expiration of the ten minutes and you would flow better.

You can easily adapt this same approach when you are engaging in preparations for an important board meeting where you have to pitch your ideas. Take a deep breath before entering the boardroom. If possible, you can engage in some mind-calming exercises and then walk boldly into the room. Before you begin, scan the room and then begin to speak without pausing for ten minutes. Generally, if this is your first run in the park, the board members may offer a few reassuring smiles as they know what you must be feeling. Keep going for the ten-minute mark and then realize that your fear is nothing but an illusion.

Embrace Imperfection Of Things (For Perfectionists)

One of the most upsetting things about our societal culture is that we tend to esteem perfection a little too much.

We hold these elaborate pageants events where we hand the crown of perfection to one person who we call the most beautiful as though others are not worthy to hold the crown. In the same vein, magazines such as Vogue and others continue to bring out their lists of Sexiest women in the world with the undertone that some women are not beautiful.

On a daily basis, new products are being churned out with the claim of being the perfect cure for this or the product to help you achieve the perfect that. Hence, we begin to see products promoting finer hair, smoother legs, smarter beards, and others.

The Perfectionist culture would be the apt description that we can give to our society. While it is okay seeking perfection, we must understand that we may never achieve such perfection in many areas of our lives.

Why this may seem like a mentality that promotes mediocrity, it is one that would help you enjoy the life you life while being content. The idea that someone is perfect does not necessarily mean that the person is perfect. This is because the word "perfect" is a relative word that differs according to location. While the culture of America may esteem the slim, pretty model as the ideal of perfection, other cultures of other parts of the world may esteem other features such as the length of hair and also the wideness of the lips.

The idea that is being espoused here is that you should be the one defining what perfection for yourself is. If you allow the society to define perfection for you, you may end up chasing after a shadow that you may never catch up with all throughout your life. The ideal image of an extraordinary life as painted by the media is when you are rich enough to own your personal jet and yacht which you can use to ride off to your personal island. The message they sell is that everyone can reach that kind of success and become extra-ordinary while forgetting that no one is superb when everyone has the same kind of wealth.

It should be taught to children that they are awesome even if they come second place at a spelling bee competition and they still retain their charm if they do not come within the first three positions when they are in their ballet classes.

Every reader who understands this principle will recognize the need to take a pause on most of their aspirations because such aspirations arose as a result of what the society defined as success. Parents who innocently tell the kids to face the 'real world' and look for 'real jobs' have killed the dreams of many kids. Many a dream have died because the parent refused to support the child in the career path since the job does not fit into the traditional kind of jobs that bring in the big bucks. At the moment, there are people who make money from being professional video gamers. These top-notch video gamers began to follow their passion at an early age and did not listen when society told them to "grow up." Some of the gamers are hired on a multimillion dollar commission by video game companies, who contract them to test their games and give positive reviews to the millions of video-gamers who follow such professionals. They recognized early that they were never going to fit into other people's definition of 'perfect' and began to follow their own passion.

The question this book is asking you today is,

Are you following your dreams or trying to achieve the perfect dream of society?

If your answer is Yes, then you will not feel the need to procrastinate since you actually love what you are doing. On the other hand, you will often procrastinate if you are chasing what society has defined as perfection.

Learn To Reward Yourself For Small Achievements

People who tend to work themselves into becoming tired without rewarding themselves often find themselves frustrated and begin to engage in procrastination if such a task comes again.

Why is this so? The answer relates to the fact that everyone loves to be rewarded.

I want you to try an experiment with your canine friend if you have one as a pet. First, set up a doggy course for her and then do her work towards scaling through every hurdle. Try and maintain silence when she comes back with the prize and then note her reaction as you walk away. Then, the next day, set up the same task and when she comes back with the same prize, shower her with lots of praise words as well a favorite and then take notice of her reaction once more. What you will immediately notice is that she would exhibit a better reaction than the previous day because of your reward for her efforts, and her confidence levels will rise.

The reason why you are probably being frustrated and postponing stuff is that you do not appreciate yourself enough. When was the last time you truly had a vacation and went with your family?

Your answer to this either showcase why you have been so grumpy and procrastinating stuff OR why you have been brimming with much confidence and attacking newer tasks with confidence.

In this age of technology that can link us in a second and make us feel as though we never left office, it is possible to be on vacation and at the office at the same time. That is why you should learn how to be on vacation truly and then switch off your devices.

If you have been procrastinating on building your love relationship and it is deteriorating, I believe a vacation should be in the cards from this time of reading. Now, I can feel that your mind is beginning to conjure up a million and one reasons why you will not be able to go; procrastination at its destructive best.

I can vividly hear those thoughts telling you,

You cannot go on a vacation at this point in your life

You will not be granted an audience when you approach your boss for it

Where would the kids stay?

That co-worker of yours at the office would bungle stuff and give trouble

Your bills are too much. How can you afford it?

You would not look good in the sun with your body out.

Would your partner accept this offer of vacation?

I can doubly assure that these thoughts if you allow them to linger, would discourage you from ever taking the step to vacation. The problem is that you think you will be richer if you shelved this kind of vacation at this time, but you are not considering the extent of refreshing that would occur if you choose to engage in this line of action. You may even be working with the wrong assumption that your superior at the office would refuse your request.

However, what if your boss at the office takes a long look at you and decides to add one more week to your vacation request? You have not thought of this because you do not understand the values that top managers place on vacations. Top Fortune 500 companies place a high premium on organizing vacations for their employees and Amazon in recent times built a gigantic edifice that they now use as offices. In the revolutionary office setting, they simulated the Amazon rainforest with the air as well as some of the animals. The reason for this is that they recognize the benefits of vacation on their employees' mindset.

If you take a vacation today as a reward, you will be physically revitalized and mentally refreshed to attack your office tasks when you return. Do not listen to the tones of negative thoughts that are encouraging you not to take a vacation. Just take a leap of faith by putting your foot on the pedal of the request.

Make A List And Counter That Feeling Of Loss

No one who has the aim of becoming successful can continue to shun the necessary first step that needs to be taken which is planning.

The Great Wall of China was first a line of thought in the mind of the Chinese emperor who began its construction. The thought must have intrigued him at the point of thought conception, but when you walk on those ancient walls, you recognize that he did not procrastinate further. Instead, he chose to write it down as well as making a list of what needed to be done. Afterward, he would have called his advisers, empire architects and every other professional who would have worked to bring the list into the reality we have at the moment. The same is obtainable for all the ancient wonders of civilization such as the Great Pyramids of Egypt, the Hanging Gardens as well as others.

Let us take the example of Facebook. While in college, Mark Zuckerberg, who was obviously a nerdy guy, identified a need that was in the community. He identified that many guys needed a medium that they could use to determine who was hot or not. This was the product that he had in his mind, but it did not stay in his mind like many ideas are lying fallow within many individuals today. Instead, he took out his paper and began to make a list of everything he needed to do before calling the necessary individuals who would provide him with the services needed in bringing Facebook to life.

Everyone has many ideas that they sometimes dismiss as not important or not feasible. As you are reading, I know you have this mind-blowing idea that you think cannot be brought into reality by the sheer grandness of it.

It may be that you are already envisioning a future where dog thoughts can be transmittable to speech and they can effectively communicate their thoughts.

You may even be thinking of a future where human beings can get an alternative source of beef that would replace the traditional cows, thus preserving the lives of animals.

There are even some individuals who have envisioned revolutionary changes in the educational sector along with revolutionary techniques that could make homelessness a forgotten reality.

For people who possess this kind of revolutionary ideas and more, there is a vital need for them to begin to put down their ideas into lists. If you took note of the examples I gave, you would notice that both the Chinese Emperor and Mark Zuckerberg began to see artists, architects that could bring their dreams into reality. The reason why it seems that you have not seen anyone that can bring your dream into reality is that you have not written it on a list. The process of doing this automatically begins to open your eyes to the possibilities around you that you may have never noticed.

For example, if you plan on developing a device that helps spinal cord victims regain their ability, you could make a list a list of what you need and then, you would be exposed to a research being carried out by NASA and some scientist using nanotechnology to help disabled soldiers regain the use of all parts of their bodies that are non-functioning.

Make Sure Your Calendar Is Filled

Calendars can become a priceless gift if you understand the best way to utilize them for your benefit. There is a wealth of functions that your calendar provides for you more than the usual reminder that it is Friday to go out with friends or your baby girl's birthday is coming up by the 10th of August. While these functions are cool. They do not encapsulate the totality of what your calendar can do. By filling up your calendar, you can be able to overcome the procrastination that is usually present when there is nothing on the calendar. This filing up of calendar remains one of the attributes of numerous high profiled professionals because they understand that a quick glance at their calendars can give them the necessary motivation that is needed to push them through the daily activity.

Beat Back Negativity With Your Thoughts

Beating back negativity will require you to build your ability to say no. It would also require you to learn the best way to engage in building up your confidence. Make no mistake about this: when you begin to succeed, the negativity will come like a storm especially from people around you who may not know your beginning. If you allow yourself to be swept by their negativity, you will end up procrastinating and not doing things that will make you rise higher. Have you ever wondered how many celebrities have remained standing despite the negativity that comes their way? It is because they were able to build a thick skin against what people said and continued to work towards getting better progressively. Often tagged as the 'Queen of Hip-hop,' Beyoncè Knowles has been able to develop a thick skin to many allegations leveled against her and Jay Z, her husband who happens to be regarded as the King of Rap.

The Power Of Positive Self-Talk

The process of avoiding procrastination involves a dire need to learn the power and pattern of positive self-talk. People who have often emerged victorious are the ones who have learned how to stimulate themselves starting from the beginning of each day. The process of saying, "I am the best" is one that is potent enough to trick your mind and position it in the right frame to face challenges. The principle of positive self-talk is something that has been proven to help boost the morale of everyone when it is time to engage in a task that seems frightening. Let us go back in history and see how Positive self-talk would have worked. Gladiators who usually fought each other would wake up on the day of the fight and begin to remind themselves that they are the best because their lives depend on it. Remind yourself that you are the best today because your future lies in it.

Letters Of Encouragement

How often do you write letters of encouragement to yourself? While that question may seem odd, it is very vital for you to ask if you are going to overcome procrastination. You will need to pen unique words of encouragement to yourself on the achievement of big milestones, and while you are chasing a particular goal. The letter format could be,

Hey Mary.

I can see that you have been putting every effort you have into finishing this project given to you by Amazon. Though the deadline is a few weeks away, I know that you can be able to pull it off because you are the best. Remember that period you were in college and completed that project for your class? Yes, you completed that project without procrastination and then ended up becoming the best in class. I know you can do it.

Go, Girl!

From Mary.

This kind of letter can be placed on the door to your fridge, or you can go to mail it to yourself if you are feeling a little bit creative.

Take Small Steps

Little drops of water make an ocean. Many have quoted popular sayings like this without understanding the meaning that is implicit within. The idea behind the quip is that you will have to start from small steps when you want to reach a goal.

If you were confronted with the task of erecting a hospital for maternity purpose in a Third World country, you would not immediately begin to erect bricks on the property you have gotten. The first step would be getting an architect who would design a structural plan for you. Often, people end up procrastinating because they took huge steps that they are not able to complete at the time and set enormous targets that are too lofty to attain. You should recognize that building anything takes time and patience. Though it looks like you are slow, take one step at a time in reaching your goal.

Self-Introspection

The process of self-introspection requires that you look inward and ask some vital questions about yourself. You can choose to engage in this process of introspection at any place provided that it is silent because noise has been proven to disrupt the quality of answers that you will arrive at.

The first set of questions that you have to ask relates to who you are and what you are going to contribute to mankind. You should be ready to answer those questions as truthfully as possible, and if you are coming up short, you could decide to go on a tour of self-discovery which should lead you to research why you were created. When you are able to ascertain your origins, the next question will be your purpose and your destination. What are you planning on giving back to mankind and where do you see yourself when you reach an advanced stage.

Eliminate The Unnecessary Task

There are a million tasks that you can do, but not all of them are important. To achieve this, you must first get a sheet where you will write out a list of the necessary things that you need to engage in order to reach the goal you wish to achieve. If you have been thinking of the best way to mend a broken relationship, you can begin by identifying the list of tasks that are going to help you. That list may go like this,

I will create time to go to the cinema with my partner.

I will ensure that I listen intently when she is speaking and respond accordingly.

I will attend counseling sessions with him.

I will make out time for the kids and help out more often.

Now, these are great tasks that will be beneficial in helping to repair a broken relationship. However, if you don't have sufficient time, you can easily scrape out the item that says that you will go to the cinema with your partner. This can be removed because the other tasks are equally important and have been proven to repair strained relationships.

Explore The Consequences Of Being Lazy; It Is The Best Mental Whip

For a long time, we have explored the possibilities and benefits of finishing a task. However, have you tried to explore the consequences of being lazy? The result of this line of action has become a better whip that drives many successful people. The reason why you are mainly procrastinating is that you do not think that your task is vital to humanity because if you do, you will realize that a lot of things will go wrong if you decide to be lazy.

It might sound pompous when we talk about humanity and procrastination in the same line but honestly, this technique will be a very very powerful one with which you will be using to displace procrastination from your daily life.

When you think about what your consequences of procrastination will be, as in like truly think, you will achieve a few things.

First, you will realize how important that task is, however odious and hateful it may be, because it impacts you and your life so much. That is the mental whip we are talking about because it becomes a propeller for the positive, driving you forward to clear what should have been cleared.

Second, you may realize, hey, that task if not done is actually not such a big deal. You will then be able to rest easy and clear that mental drag of needing to do that task away from your mind. This lets go of the accompanying guilt as well because you realize that you can effectively place this task safely in another day without procrastinating it.

Third, you may actually gain a spurt of energy and look upon the task with new lenses because of this mental practice that you just did honestly. You realize it has far reaching effects if the task is delayed, and hence your approach to it changes. Sales people may oft face this issue. Sales is always almost a weekly or monthly, perhaps yearly struggle with numbers. The salesperson needs to clock in certain numbers to qualify for commissions or even just to keep the job. However, it becomes easy to procrastinate working hard on a daily basis because a month has thirty long days. That's plenty of time isn't? And so it becomes easy to just take a break or go off early, and before you know it, the month or year is up and the numbers are shown to be lacking. If our erstwhile salesperson did this deeper introspection on the consequences of not achieving the sales, then he or she may realize that the job as well as financial rewards are at stake. Family and job security are actually on the line and this is a super important reminder daily that acts as an effective stave against procrastination.

Let us again presume that you are a doctor in an Internal Displaced person camp in a country like Somalia where there are incidents of terrorism which have led to thousands of children dying. Imagine that you choose to be lazy for one day by not attending to the dying children who are brought by their mothers. The consequence of such laziness is that many would die, and the thought that you caused it would prick your heart for a lifetime. Other consequences for people who decide to be lazy are a failure in reaching their desired goals and also shame as well.

Explore The Benefits Of Completing A Task

This is one of the best ways of beating off procrastination. When you complete a task, the first reward you get is a sense of mental ease wherein your brain is flooded with a feel-good hormone. This is the exact reverse of the above technique using the mental whip. This is actually the mental carrot so to speak.

It is invariably the thought of success and the feeling of completion of the task that will engineer feelings of happiness and fulfilment. These aren't to be scoffed at. Even if you were to just visualize doing up the task on hand, it helps with the mental picture and actually triggers the impetus to achieve it.

Humans are often visual creatures, so painting that mental picture of task accomplishment will invariably lead to a higher chance of getting it done. This is then particularly reinforced when that feeling of satisfaction and happiness on getting the job done and seeing something completed is felt. This acts as a positive anchor and again, leads one on a positive spiral away from procrastination.

Imagine how scientists feel when they come up with the final antidote to a vaccine that has been ravaging humankind like malaria? That feeling of happiness cannot be recreated in any other occasion.

Another benefit that you stand to get is that you walk gallant with a feeling of self-pride. The ability to stick to a task, from the beginning to its very end, showcases a sign of mental maturity that brings you immediate respect from everyone around who may have seen you during the course.

Shorten Your Daily To-Do List

Why do you need to clog your daily To-do list with numerous activities that you may never get to finish? Many people often make this mistake of filling their list with wonderful activities they would love to attend to during the day, but they end up frustrated when they do not finish up with such activities. When such people finish such activities, however, they become so much physically and mentally fagged out that there is no fresh vigor that remains for them to face the next day. Instead of filling your day with numerous activities which may be awesome and burdensome, pick out a few and make sure you attend to them fully while leaving the other tasks for the next day. In this way, you would have conserved your energy for attacking the tasks the next day.

Have An Accountable Person

To avoid any kind of Procrastination, cultivate the habit of having a person that you are accountable to. Accountability is a culture that is fast dying out in the present day because numerous persons do not want to hear the truth in its ugly form. Most people are developing applications that would show the popularity of other people such as Instagram and this continues to fuel a mentality that shuns criticism.

You need to get someone who will not hesitate to tell you the truth about your laxity in fulfilling your dreams. The accountable person must already be someone who cares enough about you and knows your dreams, but the likeness should extend towards chiding you when you are wasting time. In most occasions, I have found out that parents prove to be very accountable people because they do not hesitate to say the truth to their kids when such kids are lazy.

Seek Different Ways To Do A Task Better - Research To Counter Boredom

Do you find yourself repeating a method all over again without making any headway? Leave it! You do not have the luxury of time to keep on sticking to a particular method that is not working for you: rather, begin to devise new means of getting things done. If you are a kindergarten teacher who has been trying to make your kids behave without encountering any luck, you should begin to think of dynamic ways.

In order to adopt new ways, you will have to research wide: begin with academic journals that are available online and at the local libraries, discuss with psychologists and also read parenting books of people who have passed the hurdle of training children. You should not keep learning until you get what you desire and even when you do, you should not stick to a single method. Successful people always look for ways to make something better, and that is why they hardly have the opportunity to procrastinate.

Trick The Mind; Turn Your Task Into Play

When you watch many films on hypnosis and magic, you get to understand that the mind can be tricked and some people have actually mastered the art of doing so.

The need to trick the mind arises from the fact that it recognizes work and tags it as a boring chore and while you are working, you will recognize that some parts of your mind will urge you to go and play.

To combat this, convert your work into play and begin to have a nice time.

The first rule in converting your work into play is that you should chase what you are passionate about doing. For example, if you love to play the violin as a passion and then proceed towards becoming a violist by profession, it would be easy for you to trick your mind since you would easily enjoy the thrill of playing and getting people to appreciate your art

Learn the rubrics of hard work

Learning the rubrics of hard work is an important step you have to take in order to defeat the enemy of procrastination. What exactly are the indices that make up hard work?

Firstly, you have to understand the "No Pain, No Gain" rule which states that there cannot be any success without any pain attached. Selfies taken at the peak of Mount Everest may look awesome, but they do not tell the story of the grueling journey that was taken to reach the top. Numerous pop stars who show off pictures of their cars as well as magnificent mansions on 'My Crib' that is aired on MTV Base, usually do not tell the stories of the pain they underwent in order to gain their wealth.

Leverage On Your Best Ability And Skills

We have reached the section on leveraging, and we are starting off with the principle of leveraging on your best ability and skills. Leveraging is from the root word 'leverage' which generally means to take advantage of something.

You have been born with a unique set of skills that you will have to discover on your own, and early discovery of these skills will help you leverage on them. Most people procrastinate because they find themselves engaging in jobs that they are not making use of their best skills: It is just like a lawyer who is stuck on being a janitor.

When you discover your skills, you will have to use it in advancing your career and not merely sit at one spot while life walks past. If your best skills are in Networking and business, you should not remain any longer in the teaching profession because you will grow increasingly frustrated while not achieving anything.

Optimize your environment

The environment you are could make or mar your productivity and your ability to beat procrastination. More attention should be placed on social media and technology that may prevent you from doing what you need to do when you need to. For instance, your email or messenger keeps beeping to alert you of an incoming message. Social media could keep you off track of your goal, and receiving phone calls when you ought to perform a task can lead to procrastination.

Instead of this, you should schedule a significant amount of time for working on a particular task, close your IM and email, and switch off your phone (or you could turn on the "Do Not Disturb" mode and put it out of sight). Transform your environment to the one that encourages you to complete the task at hand, not the one that promotes distractions. So, don't get on the web until the task has been completed.

Leverage On People By Building A Network

The second step is leveraging on people. To leverage on people, you must first understand that you cannot do everything on your own even if you have all the skill set in the world.

The concept of leveraging on people is that you reach out to people who are good in other aspects of life and then get them to help you deal with the same challenges that you are facing. Steve Jobs understood the principle of leveraging perfectly as he was able to build teams of coders while he was not a coding genius.

The Network Marketing industry runs on the principle of leveraging because they understand the need for humans to build teams that are channeled towards success. Get out of your comfort zone and begin to network today: thankfully, LinkedIn remains one of the best platforms that you can meet professionals in order to network.

CHAPTER 4 :
WHEN IS PROCRASTINATION GOOD?

This question may sound quite odd to a large number of people. First, because it assumes that at some point, procrastination is good; and secondly, because it suggests that since procrastination can be good, it shouldn't be totally disregarded. Most of those in this category have, at one point or the other, found procrastination to be a helpful tool but may not be able to attribute those incidents to procrastination. For most, procrastination is a means to an end. However, the end determines whether or not procrastination is good or bad. While some people would naturally avoid procrastination generally and seek ways to truncate it in their life, there are people who seek ways of harnessing procrastination to accomplish certain goals effectively. Life comprises of ups and downs, and in life, there are no absolutes: the peculiarities of what we encounter daily determine the best approach hence there is no one solution fits all. There is a generally negative perception about procrastination which is unwholesome as most of the evaluation of procrastination as a concept is lopsided. Procrastination has a lot of benefits that many often overlook due to their personal bias or perhaps an oversight. For instance, procrastination stimulates creativity in a person. This is obvious because you process information faster when you are quite comfortable. You tend to really get the best out of yourself when you are "put under the spotlight," i.e., when the deadline is rapidly approaching; an individual who has a strict approach against procrastination will likely not really get to see himself in the full extent of his creative capabilities. If you are conversant with sports for example, you would realize that the urgency and intensity of the losing team gets higher as the match draws to a conclusion and need I say that there have been many instances of the losing team turning over the outcome of the match after being in a losing position earlier in the same game!

There are indeed times when procrastination is good. In fact, there are certain times when you necessarily need to procrastinate on some activities in order to be taken seriously. Imagine turning in your final year research project in college 4 weeks after commencement, no matter how brilliant your findings are and no matter how authentic they are, be rest assured that even if your supervisor would accept it, he would do so with a lot of skepticism perhaps thinking you might have simply gone to plagiarize someone else's work; even if you had produced exact findings 4 months later, he would have been more convenient with the submission coming in after 4 months than it coming after 4 weeks. Procrastination is certainly not as bad as people make it seem. Procrastination forms a huge part of leadership. Imagine a leader who makes a decision at every possible second without ruminating over the possible consequences of his decision! Certainly, a lot of hush decisions would be taken which the individual will later come to regret later on in life.

The principle of procrastination is directly connected to the principle of patience. Certainly, if you ruminate over the decisions you have taken in your life over the past few years, there would be some you have wished you have exercised a little patience over. It is easier to make bad decisions in a hurry than it is to make good ones. This is why procrastinators tend to make better decisions than those not given to procrastination, after all, they have more patience. Have you ever sat to reason about something and after a while new perspectives about that which you were thinking about begins to surface in your mind? Am sure you must have encountered this experience before. Indeed, there are times in life decisions have to be made in split seconds, and there are times when decisions have to be made in patience. However, the bigger decisions in life such as who to marry, where to live, how many children to have, what job to take up, etc. are decisions that necessitate deep thought because they would certainly have major impacts in your life both presently and in the future.

In this chapter, we would consider several instances where procrastination in doing a particular thing or making a particular move has proven to be productive to the individual.

Work-Related Procrastination

While we have agreed that procrastination may result in a loss at work or distrust, it is also important to point out that procrastination usually has its perks as well, especially in work environments. For example, intentionally delaying the submission of a report in order to perfect it could result in the detection of a miscalculation or a mistake that may have affected the general performance of the company. In this case, something naturally considered being a bad trait serves a good purpose and functions well in the collective growth of a work environment.

Also, putting off for later what can be concluded today, has its own way of keeping open an opportunity for adjustments and corrections in that particular work. For example, while working with data which is immediately computed once a particular button is clicked, an individual might decide to put off the clicking of that button to later and may, in the long run, find that there are other parts of the data which he did not enter initially and enter them promptly before finally clicking the button. We find that this saves one a lot of stress and time and helps to ensure that one's work is always accurate when crosschecked.

Academic Related Procrastination

Quite a number of times, procrastinating on the execution of a particular task resulted in the discovery of new data or detail related to that task, which in turn contributed to the betterment of that particular task. For example, a student who is writing his thesis and decides to put off the writing of the abstract until later, may find that writing the abstract by the time the entire body of work is complete is a lot more efficient because, this time, it is easier to make reference to the work which has been already completed and be accurate with it. Many students would testify that at several points through their educational process, they have found additional information to make their work better just because they delayed a little bit. In the long run, it boils down to how one manages procrastination and the possibility of harnessing procrastination to work for you successfully.

Procrastinating the Setting up of a Business

We all have that one friend who has had a business idea since we have known them but have not set up that business, largely because of procrastination. In some contexts, it is bad procrastination: for example, when the procrastination is out of fear of failure or lack of self-confidence. In other contexts, like in this one I am about to elaborate on, procrastination can be harnessed to ensure safety and effectiveness. For example, an individual who has amassed all the necessary tools and machinery for setting up a business but procrastinates the setting up of that business may be considered to be foolishly frightened. However, it could be a wise decision, especially when you consider why the individual is holding back. It might be that they do not feel like the research they have carried out on the business is not sufficient and as such need to go back to the drawing board and rectify most of the calculations made. Also, in the time of the procrastination, the individual could carry out necessary investigations and research and come up with a more failsafe solution to the problems the business seeks to solve.

Especially in business, people need to learn to harness procrastination as a tool and instead of using the term "procrastination," they could be making "calculated decisions." When people learn to harness procrastination and come to the point where they know the fine line between disinterest and bidding time, then things begin to flow a lot more easily.

In this context, there is the possibility of contrasting this reality of careful decision making with hurried executions. Both are effective ways of establishing different businesses, but one is a lot more carefully thought out and pays a lot more attention to detail.

Procrastinating Romantic Relationships to pursue Business or a Career

For some, nothing is more important than a successful career or establishing a successful business. Not even a romantic relationship. Throughout history, we have seen examples of people who were so focused on their grind that they didn't really see the need for a romantic relationship. Worthy of note is Jesus of the Christian faith which is even quoted to have said: "My meat is to do the will of him that sent me…" (John 4:34). If you follow the story of Jesus closely, you will find that he spent all of his time spreading his gospel, teaching, feeding and healing the sick, poor, dejected and lost and yet, when he was once told that his mother and brothers were looking for him, he replied that his family was every one of the people who followed him everywhere.

In our modern world, there are a lot more relatable stories or instances similar to that of Jesus, in which people have verbally or mentally declared that they would rather dedicate their life to grow a personality or brand or a business than to settle down and build a family with someone they share an emotional feeling with.

While some of these people are just worried about being unable to combine work and romance efficiently and equally scared of the prospects of breakups, some others just do not care for any of those and have successfully convinced themselves that this path requires them and them alone (or them and the few people who are willing to build with them). These last set of people work assiduously, week in and out and return home after several long hours out, to an empty apartment and a constant reminder that the life they are building doesn't require a crowd to build.

In the same vein, there are some in this category who find romantic relationships very endearing but are unable to sustain them. A typical example is Elon Musk of SpaceX who has divorced his wife with whom he had five sons and broken up with two other girlfriends. According to Musk, he needs to feel and express love in order to be at the top of his game. However, Musk hasn't been the best of the best as a romantic partner or a father, especially with making time out to spend some quality time with his loved ones. Once noting himself that he handles relationships almost perfunctorily like business meetings, Musk may have successfully procrastinated emotional feelings which are a normal human trait in exchange for a successful career or business.

Some other celebrities and big names fall under this category of people who procrastinate settling down in a relationship or in marriage because of their need to focus entirely on building their career or brand to its peak. Some of them may give the excuse of being unable to fit their attention span into building their career or business or brand and building a relationship. For some, combining the two means, one has to be boring, and when one is boring, they may be tempted to procrastinate in the boring one. And it's usually the relationship that suffers. Quite a number of female celebrities have outrightly declared that they do not need love because they were focusing on building their career and in context, they may be right. A relationship may be too much distraction for them; a relationship may be too cumbersome for them and, as we have pointed out earlier, most cases of procrastination results from the fear of venturing into something because it may be too tasking. It is safe to say that these people have mastered procrastination whether consciously or subconsciously to their benefit or to the benefit of building their desired enterprise.

Sixty-four-year-old Oprah Winfrey, for example, has been in a relationship with her partner Stedman Graham for over twenty-five years after having dated Roger Ebert in the mid-80s. To many relationship experts, this relationship hasn't been progressive for the obvious reason that it has not led to something more elaborate, like a marriage. However, we all know how successful Oprah's career has been in that time. In contrast with her relationship, her career has grown exponentially by more than one hundred and fifty percent. While it can be said that Oprah Winfrey has been unable to make reasonable headway in her relationship with Stedman Graham, it can also be said that she has successfully procrastinated the prospect of getting married for the purpose of focusing her time, attention and energy on building her brand. Whether consciously, subconsciously or unconsciously, Oprah's is another wonderful example of putting procrastination to good use.

However, we are faced at this point by the question of "who defines what is a good use?". And, even though the answer is a straightforward "the person(s) directly involved," it may still require a little or a lot of explanation to put it in context. For example, who determines that Oprah's decision is the best decision for her? And the simple answer is; herself and anyone else directly involved (in this case, Stedman). In this sense, we can bring in the question of who decides when it is right to get birth control in a marriage between a man and his wife? And the simple answer is, the persons involved. As a result, we can queue in the man and his wife. If a man was to blow up in anger due to his wife making that decision of her own accord, he wouldn't be acting out of place.

Another classic example of people procrastinating relationships in order to focus on their career is Trey Songz, who is most popularly known for his incredibly composed love songs. Trey is recorded to have mentioned once that when he is in love, he prioritizes all of his attention to loving and procrastinates his musical endeavors. Speaking with Madame Noire in 2014, the singer noted that he was all about the music and was putting all of his attention into making wonderful music.

With over 50 million albums sold, nine Grammy awards and performances with some of the best in the world, including Michael Jackson, The Rolling Stones, Prince, Kid Rock and Eric Clapton, one would wonder what it is that makes Sheryl Crow unable actually to settle into a relationship or marriage. While she has been involved in some high profile relationships, the 54-year-old has been single since she ended things with Lance Armstrong whom she was once engaged to in 2006.

Sheryl Crow, Oprah Winfrey, Elon Musk and every other celebrity or business mogul out there who have sacrificed a thriving relationship or the prospect of a thriving relationship to procrastination are examples of instances where procrastination can be used to a good effect. As long as we agree that good in this context is subjective to the persons involved.

In quite simple terms, many people want to focus more of their attention on building their brand or career, and when anything comes up that may portend a threat to the success of their endeavor, there is a subtle desire to procrastinate the development of that thing in order to keep on track with their desired endeavor.

When you have to choose your relationship over your workplace

The decisions you make determine your life outcomes. We are all a bundle of decisions, and our present state is a direct reflection of the decisions we have taken in times past. For instance, a doctor is so called because he/she had taken a decision to enroll in the medical school several years ago to obtain the necessary training and instruction relevant to becoming a doctor and likewise an engineer is so called because he/she had taken the necessary training in becoming an engineer. Two of the most important aspect in life are work and relationships. Somewhere along the life of every individual, these two factors must feature.

Man is a relational being and naturally craves affection from another member of his species. Likewise work is very important because it is a means of acquiring the resources relevant to survival in life. This is why who to marry and where to work are very critical decisions that cannot or shouldn't be taken in a hurry. At some point, it is normal for an individual to crave the emotional or romantic feeling of another individual usually a member of the opposite gender. At some point as well after school it is expected that the individual begins to seek gainful employment from which he would seek to make ends meet and finally secure financial and economic independence from his parents, caregiver or benefactor; yet as critical as these two decisions are to a person's overall welfare and wellbeing, at times there may be a conflict of interest arising as a result of a dissonance between these two important decisions.

What this means is that your relationship at times may impact your performance in the workplace and vice versa. While it is true that society places a lot of expectation on the individual particularly along the lines of our specific gender, it is, therefore, normal to be influenced by others while making decisions about our own lives while ignoring a very important principle of life which is human differences. For instance, a young couple with a kid who is just 2 years old both working at places that warrant they leave home in the morning and return later in the evening. At one hand, they are making good money which would afford them the privilege of obtaining a higher standard of living for themselves and their child, but at the same time, the demands of their jobs condemn them to be away from the child so much that they miss out on the formative years of the child.

In this instance, there is a need for deep introspective thought about the right step to take because this is a big decision that does not just affect themselves as a couple but now affects their child as well and they would be aware that whatever decision they settle upon then there would be some sort of sacrifice to be made because it is either one of the couples resigns from work to be able to spend time with the child and this would certainly result in lesser income for the family or they both maintain their work while they sacrifice the quality time they could have spent with their child in return for more money to afford the good things of life for themselves and their family. In instances like this, there are no definite answers and certainly no hasty answers. The pros and cons had to be weighed in the balance and whatever conclusions reached and decisions made would hitherto lead to happiness or regret later on in future. In situations like this, what is most important to you, therefore, takes prominence.

Scale of preference

This is perhaps the most important in economics mainly not so much because of its importance but rather because of its relevance. Even if you are unfamiliar with the concept of the scale of preference you would still have to utilize it unconsciously at some point later in your life. Getting a car is one of the dreams of everyone especially the young folks. It is such a big aspiration because it represents an upgrade in the perceived social, economic status of the individual. By all means, having a car is good because it gives you comfort and with the possession of a car, you are able to determine your own movements without recourse to anyone. Many see buying a car as a personal reward for themselves having toiled and worked for the money with which they purchased the car. However, there's something I have noticed among young employees, and that is the confusion in whether to go for real estate or to purchase a car. Without a doubt, both prospects are enterprising and are both money well spent in both instances albeit depending on the particular circumstances going for a car might be better than going for a house and vice versa.

Should I get a car now or should I just invest the money in real estate? These two options are quite okay in their own rights and depending on your age and experience; one option may appeal more to you than the other. However, I always recommend procrastination in the case of buying a car, rather than going for a car; the individual might consider investing it in a way that it can yield even more profit for the owner. The difference between the rich man and the poor man is the decisions they made in times past. Majority of the current billionaires especially the young ones had the opportunity of just splashing the cash on expensive trinkets and showing off, but they rather invested in order to have more because investment is far better than a liability. There is a need to picture yourself as a CEO, and your life is the organization you are running and then begin to make decisions that are designed towards meeting your goals; if you can adopt this mindset, certainly there will be a positive difference in your life. The major reason for my preference of real estate is motivated by the fact that it can appreciate which a car is more likely going to depreciate in value in the coming years.

Furthermore, the real estate industry is seasonal in nature in that there are times where properties come at an appealing, i.e., lower price, and this price fluctuates hence if an individual encounters such scenario, the best thing is to invest and possibly sell when the price is higher. This implies that financially, real estate appreciates while vehicles depreciate in value. Vehicles have no such season because their prices are more stable over a period of time as compared with real estate.

Go for that vacation now

We all have an option at every point in our lives. The student has an option whether to participate in tests and examination or not. The employee has an option whether to report at the office or not etc. However, the big part of it all is that no matter the decision we adopt there will be consequences at the end. I believe life is meant to be enjoyed and whenever the opportunity beckons to rest or go on vacation, we should take it with both hands. You have only one life to live, and it is better than you make good use of it. Every day as you go to work or school or whatever activity you are engaged in, your brain goes to work as well. Remember that the brain is the site of thinking in the brain, vacation gives us an opportunity to rest and recharge, to de-stress and replenish lost energy.

Vacation is one of the things that should not be procrastinated on. We all need money, but some in desperation continue to work while they were supposed to be resting. The body may not react now, but by the time it reacts, later on, the consequences may be so sudden and tragic. You might not know, or you know and perhaps don't attach more significance to it but health is wealth, treating yourself right entails you have time for work, and you have time for relaxation. The love for money must not supersede the love for self because if something inimical or untoward should happen then even the organization would easily employ another person to take your place. Such is life, and this is why I always recommend that we put ourselves first at all times. Enjoy life and have fun. Work and play!

CHAPTER 5
FAQ TO HALT PROCRASTINATION

Right now, I'm sure we are all aware that man, i.e., the human being is in a constant struggle, not with anyone but with himself. The struggle is with his instincts and desires. Procrastination occurs whenever there is a clash between the instincts and desires. Indeed, we have all procrastinated at some point in our lives; either due to stress or laziness, we have all at some point put off activity or two which could have done now till much later. Procrastination is not age specific as everyone is prone to it regardless of socio-demographic factors such as age and gender hence the prevalence of it is general and not skewed in any way. There is no one solution fits all approach for ending procrastination. It can be a sign that you are currently engaged in an activity that you are not particularly interested in because when you are passionate about a thing, the tendency to engage the activity on time is high. This is why it is a statement of fact to posit that our level of procrastination is a reflection of our preference and sense of value and interests in life.

A lot has been said procrastination which certainly would throw up some questions. Here are some of the most frequently asked questions on halting procrastination.

1. Are there any benefits to procrastination?

This is a somewhat tricky question, but I will say YES: Procrastination does have a benefit as it helps you reduce anxiety! However, procrastination in helping you reduce anxiety about a particular activity only ends up delaying the evil day. In most cases we procrastinate because we are anxious about a particular activity we should have engaged in right away, or we procrastinate because we feel the deadline for that activity is still far away or perhaps the activity in question is a personal one hence we are accountable to only ourselves in getting the activity done. Whatever the reason for procrastination, it helps us reduce our anxiety for that activity but what we get is only a temporary reprieve as the activity postponed will not go away and by procrastinating it the task to be done might get bigger as the days go by. Take for instance a student who should read daily but will rather procrastinate reading till when exams are around the corner, then the bulk of what to be covered then keeps increasing, so much that he might not be able to effectively cover every aspect of the lesson note which would have been possible had he started reading earlier.

In some cases, it has also been reported that procrastination helps improve efficiency and performance. The awareness of deadline for an activity automatically boost the concentration levels of some people and ultimately increase their concentration and output in the said activity. However, as stated earlier, there are tasks that tend to increase further if delayed hence an individual who is attuned to always procrastinating may eventually encounter a task that will overwhelm them in the nearest future. I once witnessed a situation whereby a student collapsed during the examination period. Obviously, he had taken up too much work more than he could handle and his system couldn't process it all hence he had a total breakdown. In short, procrastination helps reduce anxiety, but it is merely a Greek gift to yourself that will only come back to affect you in the nearest future adversely.

2. What is the source of procrastination?

There are many factors that could evidently trigger or motivate you to procrastinate. For instance, you are likely to procrastinate when you have no interest in an activity. The lack of interest in that activity kills your motivation and interest so much that you continue to postpone the activity until the last possible minute. In some cases, you may be overwhelmed by the size of the project that you don't know how to start and in yet some cases the perfectionist mentality in you may motivate you to wait for 'the perfect time' to begin and in anticipation of starting at best possible moment you may find yourself delaying the task.

Furthermore, nature and nurture can be complicit in the explanation of procrastination. It may sound a bit weird, but it is true that procrastination can be inherited. A person does not just inherit the biological components of their parents alone, a person may also inherit the behavioral tendencies of such parent(s) as well, and these tendencies could possibly include procrastination. The environment a person is nurtured also plays a role. A child brought up by a permissive parent is more likely to procrastinate because he/she is raised in an environment whereby there is no consequence for the adverse behavior. Hence he develops the tendency to lay off tasks meant to be done now till much later. Psychologically, the behavior is motivated by reward or reinforcements while behavior is discouraged by punishment. In a scenario whereby a child is reprimanded for procrastinating all the time, he will likely seek to do things a little bit faster just to avoid the reprimand of the parent, teacher or caregiver. Where there is no consequence for procrastination, then the behavior tends to continue unabated. This is why in seeking to investigate the reasons for your procrastination you need to evaluate the source of it.

3. Is there a link between self-control and procrastination?

Absolutely! A big part of procrastination is lack of self-control. They are like Siamese twins that cannot be separated because they go hand in hand. A chronic procrastinator has lost control of his or her own actions. The normal thing is for an individual to master himself at all times. In fact, regardless of the activity or endeavor, an individual is engaged in, self-mastery is a necessity for success and achievement. It is a necessary attribute and requirement for success because in most cases success involves self-denial and this can only come through mastery of self. Procrastination comes naturally to people who do not have the discipline to complete tasks on time. This is why any curative or preventive remedy for procrastination needs to develop a viable way of helping the client gain mastery of his own actions. This is simply non negotiable in the quest to combating procrastination.

Every form of addiction is invariably a lack of self-control. This is why the danger of procrastination is great because since procrastination is the aftermath of lack of control which is also a strong causative factor for addictions, it, therefore, follows that an individual engrossed with procrastination will likely have an addiction. Every addiction starts with a step and the individual upon realizing the danger in the activity he is engaging in could easily have stopped successfully but rather than stop straight away, he/she postpones stopping till later on until they eventually develop a dependent relationship with whatever substance or activity they are addicted to. Procrastination is also significant because it can mess up the psyche of a person and affects other aspects of their life.

I have discovered that one of the best ways to live life is to set targets for each day and work assiduously to achieve all the targets set out for the day without exception. I have discovered that the easiest way to gauge the level of control you have over your own life is to set daily targets and see how you are able to perform in the actualization of these targets. Self-indulgence is an enemy of progress because it absolutely adversely affects a person's output in any given activity. A self-indulgent person will always perform lower than expected in tasks or where they perform reasonably well in the set tasks will ultimately find it a bit difficult to meet p with the deadline set for the task. Success is strongly connected to control, and every individual must seek to take control of his or her own life and actions on a daily basis.

4. Can procrastination affect my relationships and personal life?

Behavior is transient; this is why a behavioral disposition of an individual in activity will always reflect in the other aspects of their lives. It is true that procrastination can cost you relationships with people especially loved ones and associates at work or at school, How many homes have been broken due to lack of quick resolution when disagreements arise between the couple? How many careers have been lost due to lack of quick resolution? Heck, many have even lost their preferred romantic partners due to their inability to declare their interest on time. Procrastination is so significant it can break down key relationships that could have been helpful to the individual both in the short and long run. When a partner in a relationship be it romantic, or business relationship often procrastinates, the effect is mostly that the other party feels unimportant and undervalued and they may, therefore, determine to seek an exit from such relationship. The relationship is hard work because it requires regular input consistently for it to stand. It is like a building. It requires regular input before it can grow to the desired level but unlike a building which can be stopped whenever it is complete, there is always need to put in more effort into a relationship at all time because the day you stop putting in effort into a relationship is the day you're your partner begins to lose value and worth in your eyes and is the day that relationship begins to die.

Every activity or task we engage in daily so far as it entails interaction with people, we build a relationship. You must have heard the quote first impression matters a lot. Picture a situation of a job interview whereby a particular applicant meets all the criteria's listed out as a prerequisite for the job, but the individual comes late for the job interview. While the fellow might have cogent reasons for his lateness, he or she has ultimately created a wrong perception of himself and has therefore started out a potential relationship on a wrong footing. There are many qualified applicants who are discounted merely on the basis of punctuality yearly. This is why it is very true that procrastination can affect not just a person's life but also their relationship with others. I guess it is, therefore, safe to say that your happiness may be connected to the promptness at which you take up tasks.

5. Are Procrastinators bad people?

Procrastinators are not necessarily bad people. In fact, in most cases, they often turn out to be nice and caring people who are easy to mingle with and relate with others around them. On a personal level, procrastinators, are merely those who like putting off tasks till much later, and this does not in any way tamper with their relational or interpersonal skills. They are just like every other person. They are as easy to mingle with, and just anyone could readily relate with someone given to procrastination. Strangely, procrastinators are always fun to be around. They are mostly calm and collected as they have a relaxed approach towards life. They are the ones usually cracking jokes and bringing about a relaxed atmosphere when there is a task to be done. They emphasized work and play which is why they are usually nice to be around.

However, on a professional note, they may not be the best of partners to have whether as a colleague at work or as a partner working on a group assignment in school. Procrastinators always contribute little to the group task and group goals. The reason for this is pretty obvious. They are less productive at what they do and in the most cases always exceed deadlines hence while they may be friends with everyone on a personal level, they may not necessarily be the darling of everyone when it comes to official or professional assignments. This is because they may weigh everyone down with their laid-back approach to work. At times, they are perfectionists, and they influence people around them with their calm demeanor.

6. What are the dangers of procrastination?

You must understand that overindulgence in procrastination often come at some costs to the procrastinator. It can lead to broken relationships because it can throw up a feeling of lack of worth or relevance in the mind of the other party that can make them unhappy and perhaps seeks a separation. This I believe is the biggest danger of procrastination. This is because they may feel that perhaps the other party is cheating on them since they don't seem to value them again hence there must be someone else in the picture even if he or she is hidden somewhere. A simple analysis of some of the divorce cases around today has elements of procrastination in them not just because in terms of their refusal or inability to settle rift on time but also due to their oversight generally on issues pertaining to themselves as a couple. Issues on love and relationships are quite important in life; it is a huge emotional investment which we will all make at some point in life which is why both parties involved must always keep the other happy by putting their interest and happiness at the top of their own agenda.

It can lead to career setback because a procrastinator will likely have issues with punctuality at work as well as complying with deadlines on a particular issue. All of which can affect the reputation of the employee with his/her employers. In fact, it can lead to isolation in the office especially when it comes to tasks requiring collective effort; past history of abdication of duty often comes to mind and may lead to the person being sidelined by others around them. Career-wise, it may be unwise to have the habit of procrastinating. The truth is that consecutively missed deadlines will always have a negative impact on the professional life of the individual whether in the short run or long run.

For a student, procrastination can negatively affect academic performance. When the students continuously postpone reading and resolving assignments; the end result might not be good enough. For the entrepreneur, procrastination can result in an inability to meet up with deadlines and targets, and this could hamper the relationship between the entrepreneur and client and this can eventually lead to a decline in income. For the average individual, procrastination can lead to deterioration in health when the individual continuously put off the healthy foods, exercising and sleep till much later, it could lead to deterioration of health and even sicknesses and disease as well as death in some extreme cases. The essential point to note is that procrastination affects output because for example, when an assignment is given in class and due for submission within the next 24 hours, procrastinating on getting the assignment done will result in the time left continuously shrinking and decreasing so that when the individual is ready to tackle it he will have to do it in a hurry, and this will certainly affect the quality of work done.

Procrastination can cause anxiety as well. Take the instance of household chores, for example, you put off the task of washing dishes till much later say the next day, the dirty dishes will keep piling up and other tasks will keep joining until such individual is in a frenzy on how to clear the dirty dishes. Time is an illusion; we often think we have time when in reality we don't even have much time left again. Doing things as early as possible makes one attains some level of rest and calmness rather than running around to fulfill the task later on. It is imperative that the individual understands self and refuse the urge to compare themselves with others when it comes to their approach to resolving tasks. For instance, there are students who have the habit of reading for the exam when it is very close by and as weird as that seem they perform quite okay and excel in it, and there are yet others that don't perform well with such scattergun approach.

7. Are there ways to overcome procrastination?

If you find yourself frustrated and in desperate need of overcoming the problem, the good news is that procrastination can be overcome.

Certainly, procrastination can be conquered if you really do set your mind to do it. I must confess that it might be hard especially if you have been on it for quite a while. Speaking from experience, merely verbal confession of willingness to end procrastination is not enough. It takes concerted willpower from the concerned individual to effectively conquer procrastination for good. There are certain steps you can practice to overcome procrastination quickly, and some of them are enumerated below;

i. The first step to overcoming procrastination is the admittance that it could be bad and has a negative effect on you as a person. You cannot conquer what you do not see as bad in the first place. You must simply come to the acknowledgment of the issue as a problem and challenge that is not beneficial to you.

ii. Identify the lost opportunities and deadlines missed due to your procrastinating on some activities in the past. Doing this will give you more basis to be angry at procrastination and infuse you with the necessary strength and fortitude needed to overcome the problem.

iii. Forgive yourself for past issues that must have arisen as a result of procrastination. You need to let go of past hurts and mistakes, wipe the slate clean and start on a new page.

iv. Set daily targets: Rome was not built in a day; it was built gradually until it was eventually completed. Every big thing starts small, so if you want to overcome such a big problem as procrastination then you must start setting daily targets which you must strive to actualize; doing the small daily tasks consistently would equip you with the self-belief needed to help you to conquer the bigger tasks. Have a to-do list which would be written daily and placed at a conspicuous place where you would always come in contact with it regularly and be reminded of what still needs to be done. Approach your daily targets with accuracy and precision and ensure that no day passes by without you ticking up every item on your to-do list.

v. Reward yourself: The concept of reward is central to the principle of motivation. As you seek to drop the habit of procrastination, you should learn to reward and motivate yourself for every achievement made along the way to overcoming the problem. The reward will keep you motivated. However, due to the fact that you are the one administering the reward, avoid the temptation to abuse it by giving yourself the reward even though there are still other items on your list waiting to be achieved for the day.

vi. Minimize distractions: Distraction is the archenemy of activity. When distracted the tendency to procrastinate till when the distraction is gone often arises. Hence, in order to fully overcome procrastination; move away from people or things that form distractions to you. You need all the focus you can garner. Hence you must eschew the company of those that affect your concentration.

8. Is procrastination a reflection of my level of motivation?

Not really. Procrastination is not necessarily a good reflection or gauge of your level of motivation. At times you procrastinate out of confidence, and at times you procrastinate out of doubt about something. If as a student you are given an assignment with duration of 8 days, yet the questions seem like what you can accomplish in a day, it is normal to want to set it off till much later. Likewise, if an assignment is given which seems cumbersome and difficult, it is likely that the student will delay on the project rather than getting it done right away. In the first instance, overconfidence was the complicit factor in procrastinating the time for resolving the assignment and in the second instance lack of confidence was the factor responsible for the lack of interest in the task.

There are certain theorists that view procrastination as a personal weakness in individuals but it is clear enough in recent times that procrastination is dependent on the individual as a person and has nothing to do with it being a weakness because there are those who procrastinate and have been able to achieve as much success as even some of those who do not procrastinate. However what can be truly said of procrastination is that it is a reflection of an individual's orientation on personal enjoyment and wellbeing. A person who feels life must be enjoyed will likely value rest more than work if put in a position to make an option out of the two. This is why it is said that procrastination is a function of a mismatch between current engagement and the motivational structures that is situated in a person.

Why do you do the activity you are engaged in? Is it due to your personal interest or the expectation of parents or society? We reside in a world where you are compelled to take on some roles and activities regardless of your interests in them. You are forced to be who you really are not and is not interested in being. This often brings about a lack of motivation which usually culminates in procrastination. Interest and activity are intertwined. When you are really interested in an activity, you tend to love engaging in it naturally. This is why little children do not really need much pacifying before they play with their toys. I have realized that at times the difference between the best and the worst student in a class is not necessarily a function of the intelligent quotient levels. At times it is just out of interests. The interest one has in the course makes him read regularly even wider than the syllabus covered by the instructor while the lack of interest of one makes him disdain the studies that he merely reads and even though he possesses the capacity to be brilliant in that course, he is simply unwilling to exert himself towards becoming the best he can be.

9. Are there types of procrastinators? If yes, what type do I belong to?

Ideally and truthfully, every human being walking the earth has procrastinated at some point in his or her lives. However, the frequency at which we procrastinate is what varies. This, therefore, begs the question is there types of procrastinators and what are the types of procrastination available? This question is important because knowing your type of procrastination will certainly be of huge help in the quest to overcome the problem. There are six known types of procrastinator, and they are enumerated below;

i. Dreamers: These are the categories of people who have a laid-back approach towards life in general. They are usually narcissistic in nature and have a heightened sense of self-importance. Just as the name implies, they so much love to fantasize rather than put in work needed to achieve their often-lofty dreams.

ii. Defiers: These categories of people just like the dreamers also have a delusion of self-importance because they find it difficult to comply with instructions from a superior. They often put off tasks due to be done in the present till much later simply because they always seem to go against authority. Defying authority instructions gives them some level of intrinsic happiness within themselves because by their defiance they derive a feeling of power that serves to only boost their ego.

iii. Worriers: These categories of people are those that worry a lot after a task is given. They merely procrastinate because they feel like they are not in the best possible mood or scenario to begin the implementation of a task. Rather than begin on time, they often begin later and at times may not get to complete the task at hand. This behavior often makes them underachievers in some way because at the very end they mostly get their tasks done under duress due to the fear of impending deadlines hence they may not be able to give their best before all is wrapped up.

iv. Perfectionist: These categories of people are usually very slow in taking off. They always don't start on time. They are very similar to the worriers but their own refusal to start earlier is not down to worry but due to overconfidence or pride. They see every task no matter how insignificant as a direct reflection of their abilities hence they want to give out the best but rather than start early; they often prefer starting later.

v. Overdoers: These ones lack concentration. They have a short attention span yet they take on multiple activities simultaneously. Rather than give a task their undivided attention before moving on to other activities, they juggle multiple activities together concurrently. At times as a result of taking on multiple tasks at the same time, they may not be able to deliver on their tasks as at when due. They are mostly members of the Sanguine temperamental class that we discussed in chapter three and one profound thing about them is that they need to research in-depth to know how to be fully focused in the tasks they are given.

vi. Crisis makers: This is the category of chronic procrastinators. Their procrastination is so severe that they want to achieve what they naturally should have taken about 2 months to achieve they often seek to achieve it in a few days. Majority of those who fall within this continuum are students as it is not uncommon to meet a student trying to juggle reading his class notes and textbooks just a few hours to the exam even though he has been aware of exam coming up.

CHAPTER 6 :
CONCLUSION

As we know and can collectively agree, everything which has a beginning must come to a close at some point. For this reason, it is imperative that this book comes to a close. However, before I walk away from all I have shared in this collection of advice and direction, let us take a few minutes to refresh on the contents and points I have considered so far.

It has been established that procrastination isn't exactly a wonderful trait to have. For this reason, anyone who suffers from any form of procrastination or from the effects of procrastinating may find resource herein to help them get by to change or get better. In defining procrastination, I find that it implies putting off for later what can be done now. In a lot of situations and events, there are very visible effects of procrastination. For example, it is easy to notice the effect of procrastination in the making of laws relating to security or gun control. At the same time, it is easy to notice the effects of procrastination in making traffic and/or immigration laws. The effects of procrastination in these scenarios would show up almost immediately.

However, there are situations in which the effects of procrastination may not present themselves immediately. In some such cases, the effects only show up after severe harm has been done and to some irreversible extent. Examples include procrastination in work-related contexts, romantic and business relationships and health-related circumstances. For example, when a romantic relationship breaks apart, people without relationship experience would easily assume that the relationship broke apart by occurrences which occurred immediately before the break. However, in most cases where relationships break apart, the reasons for the break are usually more far-fetched than a simple fight the day before. Sometimes, the reason is a long overdue apology expected from a partner, or a habit which should have been rectified long ago but wasn't because "there's still time to fix this" is a common excuse people give.

In work related contexts, procrastination can have far-reaching effects years after the actual act of procrastination occurs. For example, a document a manager was too lazy to file adequately 3 years ago may get damaged over the years and cost the firm a fat contract which requires that document. In situations like this, it is safe to say the effects of procrastination are more long term than short term.

In this book, I attempted to identify procrastination, its allies and manifestations, and the overreaching effects of putting off for later, what can be done today, and the instances where procrastination can aid and lead to productive growth either in business or career. With this information, I attempted to create a reasonable solution to the problem of procrastination, through suggestions and simulations of workable and practical formulas for managing procrastination professionally to suit a specific ambition and aid that ambition to grow into a real benefit.

Some of the causes or reasons for procrastination identified include: laziness, boredom, tiredness, fear of failure, desire to be absolutely perfect, fear of success, the feeling of being overwhelmed, waiting for the right time, feeling of negativity, negative self-talk and declaration, lack of stoicism, uncertainty on whether or where to start from, indecisiveness, fear of hard work, etcetera.

Some practical case scenarios of these in work-related and general contexts include laziness to finish reports at work which may eventually lead to clutter in both your work schedule and your work table. This could, in turn, result in a loss of confidence in one's ability to execute tasks by the boss or a loss of data due to the eventual rush to complete the task later on. Either way, laziness results in procrastination which in turn results in a terrible outcome.

Similarly, a feeling of boredom may result in a severe case of procrastination. For example, a writer with a deadline for publication may be too bored with the process of writing the particular text and seek excitement in doing other things which may, in turn, result in a delay in the execution of the writing project. In the same vein, much procrastination is as a result of a lack of stoicism or a feeling of uncertainty on whether to start or where to start from. Any feeling of uncertainty could be classified among the more frequent reasons why many great ideas are not birthed. This feeling of uncertainty comes from several discouraging pointers in the process of planning for a particular idea or for the execution of particular inspiration.

Also, in this book, I outlined a number of ways through which procrastination can be beaten to the back seat or used effectively to achieve a responsible ambition. Summarily, these include; adopting a "so what" mentality in situations involving the feeling of fear of failure or fear of success. The "so what" mentality is a mechanism of the mind which sounds a rebuttal at the voice inside the head which projects the many challenges that may present themselves in the process of accomplishing a particular task. The "so what" mentality is preferable because it is a psychological response which both counters the question and reassures the mind of the individual who uses it. This mentality gives one a kind of confidence similar to the confidence gained from taking alcohol or some kinds of drugs.

Another way of combating procrastination is to make a mental or physical note of the various things you may have to do for each day and develop the habit of following through with that schedule to accomplish the tasks outlined within. For people who have to procrastinate as a result of a craving to be perfect, it helps to convince yourself that imperfections are regular and normal traits of the human nature and as such, there is nothing terrible about having imperfections in your work. Convincing the mind to believe a particular thing is easy, all it takes is an agreement to continuously remind the mind of that particular thing until it becomes a part of the mind. Another way that works is rewarding yourself for accomplishing small feats from time to time. This way, you can successfully convince your mind that accomplishing tasks at the proper time is rewarding and in turn successfully convince your mind to take new tasks seriously and work assiduously on completing them. In this book, I also found that seeking different ways of doing things helps to keep us on track and counter boredom in work-related scenarios. By choosing more interesting ways of working on a particular task, you may find the right inspiration to execute that task. For example, someone who finds music interesting and engaging may find that listening to music while working is a very efficient way of making work a lot more interesting. In this vein, when the individual feels bored with work or a particular task, they could help the situation by listening to music alongside completing the task. However, when employing this solution, be sure to remember that if what makes the individual feel interested or engaged also serves as a form of distraction, then it shouldn't be considered. For example, someone who is wont to bob his head to a song or sing along may consider using something else to avoid the distraction of pausing in the middle of completing a task just to bob to their favorite song or sing a particular line from their favorite song.

I also considered in this book that, one sure fire way of solving procrastination might be to get to the root of the actual reason for the procrastination. Many would suggest that this should come first before anything else. As we know, the quickest way to a solution is first identifying the problem. Once you have been able to point out that the problem or reason for your procrastination is laziness or disinterest or a fear of success or failure, you can then proceed to determine whether the more practical solution is a psychological approach or a physical approach (e.g., taking notes or setting reminders and creating to-do lists).

I also pointed out that another sure-fire way of overcoming procrastination is to join up a boring or monotonous task with another more interesting or pairing up a difficult task with another more pleasant or less strenuous. When very difficult and not so difficult are executed side by side, results become a lot less difficult to get.

I pointed out also that some people usually seek the help of a mentor or someone who can be considered a coach to help them with guidance through the process of executing a project. Once there is someone who cares about how much time it takes you to accomplish a task, it becomes less likely that you will procrastinate on that task. Also, mentors and coaches help you get rid of distractions and lazy man excuses and, as a result, help you achieve your set goals on each task at the estimated time. From this point, a mention was made of the importance of goal setting and goal monitoring. Setting a goal is one thing and making the conscious effort to monitor the progress of that goal is another thing. While some people complain that they find it difficult to reach or achieve their goals, they fail to realize that just setting a goal doesn't mean you won't procrastinate during the process of execution of that goal. Putting measures in place to monitor the progress of that goal is as important as setting the goal itself. Whether in the form of human reminders and watchdogs or technological watchdogs, it is important to have a contingency which keeps you in check during the process of completing a task, to avoid procrastination. Still, wonder why so many firms have project supervisors?

In chapter four, I touched on a very dicey aspect of the general topic; when is procrastination good? In the process of trying to answer this question, I first answered the question: is there any good in procrastination. While dealing with this, I find that while procrastination is popularly labeled as a bad trait, when adequately managed, procrastination can be harnessed positively to achieve a specific ambition whether in work or in a general aspect of life. I find that what most refer to as terrible human trait, others have trained themselves to use as an excuse to achieve certain levels of success. Some examples given in this chapter include the lives of successful businessmen and women or career men and women who procrastinate the notion of getting into a relationship or settling down to marriage, mostly because of their desire to attain a certain level of career and business success. I find that many such persons are considered to be romantically shut off from the rest of the world and only focus on building their business or career, when, however, they feel emotional attachments like normal people. For some of them, this procrastination isn't intentional; they just find that they keep putting off for later, an emotion that needs to be expressed now.

While I reviewed examples of people who fall into this category, I considered that for most of them, there is a more pressing urge to accomplish a work-related task than to call a loved one. As a result, there is a lot more focus on work than there is on emotional attachments. Also, I find that for most of these people, it is not the absence of a loved one but the laziness to express affection towards that person that leads to this procrastination. Also, I discover that some people have successfully learned the subtle art of postponing emotional attachment in order to reduce the burden of the individual and focus more on what adds to the achievement of their ambition. I can say these are skilled in the art of procrastination (if we agree that procrastination is basically postponing things you can do now to later).

I am sure that this book has helped you in understanding the concept of procrastination, the pros and the cons that are attached to it as well as broaden your knowledge base on how to overcome it or help others who may need to overcome it. Without a doubt, procrastination is the biggest challenge of our time. The advent of civilization has brought about widespread technological advancement that has made procrastination so appealing that it is fast taking up endemic proportions among the old and young alike. How do you feel when people delay the performance of a task you gave them until much later? Your feeling should determine your approach to procrastination. Procrastination is not absolutely bad neither can it be absolutely said to be good because it has certain benefits as well some bad sides. If you manage it well, procrastination can pretty much work well for you. The reality of life is that everything no matter what it is if done in excess will adversely affect the doer. Certainly, it is imperative that you show dedication to any task we are saddled with, and this means. The life of a human being is like a car, and the individual is the driver himself, excessive procrastination takes over the control of your life because control is at the root of procrastination.

It is quite easy to overcome it. The human being has been naturally equipped with the capacity to overcome any behavioral disposition they deem unfavorable. The possession of willpower is the biggest tool in the arsenal available to us in defeating procrastination. There are various ways in which procrastination can be overcomed, and a lot of it has already been examined at length earlier in this book. If you have been adversely affected by procrastination in the past, I am here to tell you that you can overcome. It is a fight that you can win if you are willing to fight it smartly. You can overcome, and I believe you will. However, I will advise that as a matter of urgency right now every time you wake up to set a to-do list for yourself and try as much as possible to fix a deadline for the achievements of the tasks. Make sure that you ensure due diligence in achieving the tasks. Overcoming procrastination is a battle that requires utmost discipline if you must win. If you list out your daily tasks and are able to achieve them, then you will be strengthened in your resolve to winning the grudge battle with procrastination. Ensure you reward yourself as well when you have achieved your tasks for the day. It will serve as a major motivation that will fuel your passion towards overcoming it forever. There are people that procrastinate their efforts towards ending procrastination! It is really compelling how you can procrastinate ending procrastination itself! The fact is that the best time to start if you must end procrastination is now. There is no better time or day to start than right now. If you decided to read today, after reading this book, go and read that which you planned reading earlier. In fact, if you have successfully read the contents of this book from the beginning right to this concluding part, then it is a testament that you are already half way towards overcoming procrastination and gaining back the control of your life. As soon as you set your tasks for the day, try to start immediately. You do not necessarily wait till nightfall before completing the tasks on your to-do list. Imbibing the culture of starting out a task early is very good as it helps the individual enough time to ruminate and reflect on other aspects of that task and possibly make some improvements and modification if need be before the end of the day.

Those who are used to procrastination often report their likeness for the adrenaline rush they feel like the main contributory factor towards continuing the trend. While you might develop a feel-good feeling at the prospect of achieving your tasks within a short while, it is not good to live life this way as your recalcitrant attitude will eventually catch up with you whether now or later. Save yourself the unnecessary stress by accomplishing your tasks earlier rather than waiting for much later when the time would no longer be on your side. You can compensate yourself by engaging in sports or any other similar activity that can bring you the needed adrenaline rush.

Also, you must learn to say no to distractions if you must overcome procrastination. Browsing the internet, mingling with friends and watching television have all been some of the most common distractors around. You must learn to avoid these distractors if you must accomplish your wish of overcoming procrastination. If need be, these distractors can be fixed as the medium of reward you give yourself after accomplishing your tasks for the day. Believe me; it is such a great feeling to overcome procrastination and gain control and mastery over yourself.

So far, this book has served to satisfy the longing to beat procrastination or, at least, use it effectively for a beneficial goal. What have you gotten from this book? I implore you to utilize the steps you have learned from this book as soon as possible. Also, consider picking out 9 proven ways of curbing procrastination which you most identify with and write them out on your journal or iPhone or anywhere you can easily see it to remember or as a daily reminder. This way, those tips would remain with you and find expression from within.

Use the strategies highlighted within, any of the 36 proven steps with which you can utilize to beat procrastination. Or at least turn it around such that you aren't adversely affected by it.

It is here that I have got to bid you a short good bye. And I hope to see you again in my other books - that is if I do not procrastinate on writing them! That was indeed a joke and jibe at myself.

At this juncture before you go

I would like to seek your help on a single matter of some importance.

Would you be able to share with the good folks that shop on amazon what you have picked up from this book? Any single 1 of the 36 stratagems which you took up and found particularly effective?

It would be great to let the other folks know and also to help this budding writer out a little! Actually it matters quite a bit

So here's a big Thank You in advance for this

And have a great day!

Printed in Great Britain
by Amazon